～ At a Glance

Sentences

FIFTH EDITION

Lee Brandon
Mt. San Antonio College

WADSWORTH
CENGAGE Learning·

Australia • Brazil • Japan • Korea • Mexico • Singapore • Spain • United Kingdom • United States

WADSWORTH
CENGAGE Learning

To Sharon

**At a Glance: Sentences,
Fifth Edition**
Lee Brandon

Senior Publisher: Lyn Uhl

Director of Developmental
English and College
Success: Annie Todd

Development Editor: Karen
Mauk

Assistant Editor: Melanie
Opacki

Editorial Assistant:
Matthew Conte

Media Editor: Amy Gibbons

Senior Marketing Manager:
Kirsten Stoller

Marketing Coordinator:
Ryan Ahern

Marketing Communications
Manager: Stacey Purviance

Content Project Manager:
Aimee Chevrette Bear

Art Director: Jill Ort

Print Buyer: Susan Spencer

Rights Acquisition Specialist:
Katie Huha

Production Service: Books By
Design, Inc.

Cover Designer: Walter Kopek

Cover Image: Getty Images

Compositor: S4Carlisle
Publishing Services

For product information and technology assistance, contact us at
**Cengage Learning Customer & Sales Support,
1-800-354-9706**

For permission to use material from this text or product, submit
all requests online at **www.cengage.com/permissions.**
Further permissions questions can be e-mailed to
permissionrequest@cengage.com.

Library of Congress Control Number: 2010933765

ISBN-13: 978-0-495-90637-7
ISBN-10: 0-495-90637-9

Wadsworth
20 Channel Center Street
Boston, MA 02210
USA

Cengage Learning is a leading provider of customized learning solutions
with office locations around the globe, including Singapore, the
United Kingdom, Australia, Mexico, Brazil and Japan. Locate your
local office at **international.cengage.com/region**

Cengage Learning products are represented in Canada by Nelson
Education, Ltd.

For your course and learning solutions, visit **www.cengage.com.**
Purchase any of our products at your local college store or at our
preferred online store **www.cengagebrain.com.**

Printed in the United States of America
1 2 3 4 5 6 7 14 13 12 11 10

~ Contents

Preface viii
Student Overview xiii

1 Parts of Speech 1

Nouns 2
Pronouns 2
Verbs 3
Adjectives 4
Adverbs 4
Prepositions 5
Conjunctions 6
Interjections 8
Chapter Review 8

2 Subjects and Verbs 12

Subjects 12
   Nouns 13
   Pronouns 13
   Compound Subjects 14
   Implied Subjects 14
   Trouble Spots 14
Verbs 17
   Types of Verbs 17
   Verb Phrases 17
   Compound Verbs 18
   Verbals 18
Location of Subjects and Verbs 22
Chapter Review 22

3 Kinds of Sentences 27

Clauses 27
   Independent Clauses 27
   Dependent Clauses 27

Relative Clauses   28
Trouble Spot: Phrases   28

Types of Sentences   29

Simple Sentences   30
Compound Sentences   31
Complex Sentences   32
Compound-Complex Sentences   33

Chapter Review   34

**4   Combining Sentences, Avoiding Omissions,
       Achieving Sentence Variety   38**

Coordination: The Compound Sentence   38

Punctuation with Coordinating Conjunctions   39
Semicolons and Conjunctive Adverbs   41
Punctuation with Semicolons and Conjunctive Adverbs   41

Subordination: The Complex Sentence   43

Punctuation with Subordinating Conjunctions   45
Punctuation with Relative Pronouns   46

**Coordination and Subordination: The Compound-Complex
Sentence   48**

Punctuation of Complicated Compound or Compound-
Complex Sentences 49

Other Ways to Combine Ideas   50

Omissions: When Parts Are Missing   51

Variety in Sentences: Types, Order, Length, Beginnings   53

Types   53
Order   54
Length   54
Beginnings   54

Chapter Review   55

5   Correcting Fragments, Comma Splices, and Run-Ons   59

Fragments   59

Dependent Clauses as Fragments: Clauses with
Subordinating Conjunctions   60
Dependent Clauses as Fragments: Clauses with
Relative Pronouns   60
Phrases as Fragments   61

Fragments as Word Groups Without Subjects
or Without Verbs   62
Acceptable Fragments   62

Comma Splices and Run-Ons   67
Correcting Comma Splices and Run-Ons   68
Chapter Review   76

6   Balancing Sentence Parts   **79**

Basic Principles of Parallelism   79
Signal Words   80
Combination Signal Words   82
Chapter Review   84

7   Verbs   **86**

Regular and Irregular Verbs   86
Regular Verbs   86
Irregular Verbs   88
"Problem" Verbs   91
The Twelve Verb Tenses at a Glance   92
Simple Tenses   92
Perfect Tenses   92
Progressive Tenses   93
Perfect Progressive Tenses   93
Community Dialects and Standard Usage   93
Subject-Verb Agreement   103
Consistency in Tense   108
Active and Passive Voice   112
Strong Verbs   114
Chapter Review   116

8   Pronouns   **118**

Pronoun Case   118
Subjective Case   119
Objective Case   120
Techniques for Determining Case   121
Pronoun-Antecedent Agreement   126
Agreement in Person   127
Agreement in Number   128
Agreement in Gender   129

Pronoun Reference   132
Chapter Review   134

9   Adjectives and Adverbs   136

Selecting Adjectives and Adverbs   138
Comparative and Superlative Forms   140
   Adjectives   140
   Adverbs   141
Dangling and Misplaced Modifiers   146
Chapter Review   150

10   Punctuation and Capitalization   152

End Punctuation   152
   Periods   152
   Question Marks   153
   Exclamation Points   153
Commas   153
   Commas to Separate   153
   Commas to Set Off   154
Semicolons   160
Quotation Marks   164
Punctuation with Quotation Marks   166
Italics   166
Dashes   168
Colons   169
Parentheses   170
Brackets   170
Apostrophes   171
Hyphens   172
Capitalization   172
Chapter Review   176

11   Spelling and Commonly Confused Words   179

Spelling Tips   179
Frequently Misspelled Words   182
Confused Spelling/Confusing Words   185
Wordy Phrases   191

12   The Writing Process: Paragraphs and Essays   193

The Paragraph and Essay Defined   193
The Writing Process   194

Prewriting   194
Writing a First Draft   197
Revising and Editing   198

The Writing Process Worksheet   201

13   Combined and Specific Patterns of Writing and Writing Topics   203

Combined Patterns of Writing   203
Specific Patterns of Writing   204

Descriptive Narration   204
Exemplification   205
Analysis by Division   206
Process Analysis   207
Cause and Effect   209
Comparison and Contrast   211
Definition   213
Argument   215

A Variety of Writing Topics   217

Index   219

Preface

In this, the fifth edition of *At a Glance: Sentences*, the surf writer, gallantly perched on a pencil, celebrates the "flow of writing." Like waves at a beach, writing is cyclical, moving forward and backward and forward again. As the students' guide and muse, the surf writer will always be searching for the "perfect wave," meaning the best possible expression—one that is correct and effective. The recursive maneuvers of prewriting, organization, writing, revision, and editing are the essence of that relentless search.

   At a Glance: Sentences is the first-level book in the *At a Glance* series. Along with *At a Glance: Paragraphs, At a Glance: Essays,* and *At a Glance: Reader,* it meets the current need for succinct, comprehensive, and up-to-date textbooks that students can afford. All four books provide basic instruction, exercises, and writing assignments at the designated level, as well as support material for instructors. *At a Glance: Sentences* and *At a Glance: Paragraphs* include a transition to the next level of writing. *At a Glance: Paragraphs* and *At a Glance: Essays* conclude with a handbook that students can refer to for help with sentence-level issues or for problems with mechanics. *At a Glance: Reader* presents brief writing instruction and thirty sources for discussion, modeling, and reading-based writing. Each book in the *At a Glance* series can be used alone, with one of the other *At a Glance* books, or with another textbook. Two or more *At a Glance* books can be shrink-wrapped and delivered at a discount.

Comprehensive Coverage

Using exercises, examples, and writing applications, the fifth edition of *At a Glance: Sentences*

- focuses on sentence writing, with detailed attention to matters such as grammar, rhetoric, sentence variety, sentence combining, diction, capitalization, punctuation, and spelling (Chapters 1–11);

- includes a reproducible Writing Process Worksheet designed to provide guidance for students and save time and effort for instructors (located in Chapter 12 on page 202 and on the Student Companion Site);
- presents concise instruction with student examples on the process of writing paragraphs and short essays (Chapter 12);
- and includes further instruction with more than a hundred prompts and topics for writing specific and combined patterns of paragraphs and essays (Chapter 13).

Instructional Approach for Writing Sentences

In Chapters 1–11 of *At a Glance: Sentences*, contextual exercises explore humorous, contemporary, informative, and culturally diverse topics selected to engage students' interest. Principles, rules, and guidelines are explained concisely and are supported directly with appropriate examples. Each unit of sentence writing concludes with a review consisting of additional practice, and when appropriate, directs students to write original sentences. The Instructor Companion Site provides a diagnostic test, a final examination, and unit quizzes that can be given as tests or used as additional exercises.

Instructional Approach for Writing Paragraphs and Short Essays

Using examples and concise instruction along with more than a hundred topics, Chapters 12 and 13 provide the framework for working on sentences in the contexts of paragraph and essay assignments. The writing process explains the stages of writing. Patterns of writing and combined patterns of writing help guide organization necessary for particular assignments. The acronyms CLUESS (coherence, language, unity, emphasis, support, and sentences) and COPS (capitalization, omissions, punctuation, and spelling) facilitate revision and editing for students and function as rubrics in peer-editing.

⌒ New and Enhanced Material

- Additional exercise material for sentence combining (Chapter 4)
- Additional exercise material for correcting fragments, comma splices, and run-ons (Chapter 5)
- Additional exercise material on subject-verb agreement (Chapter 7)
- Transitional words specific for eight patterns of writing (Chapter 13)
- Additional student and instructor companion site support material (online)
- Refined basic instruction in writing patterns of descriptive narration, exemplification, analysis by division, process analysis, cause and effect, comparison and contrast, definition, and argument (Chapter 13)
- Thirty-three additional topics for writing paragraphs and short essays (Chapters 12–13)
- Increased emphasis on critical thinking (throughout)
- A reproducible Writing Process Worksheet designed to provide guidance for students and save time and effort for instructors (in Chapter 12 on page 202 and on the Student Companion Site)
- Additional Reading-Based, General, Cross-Curricular, and Career-Related writing topics with a diverse range of subjects
- Opportunities for practicing new skills in topic exploration, organization, writing, revision, and editing (Chapter 13)

⌒ Special Brandon Feature at a Glance: The Writing Process Worksheet

The Writing Process Worksheet provides a flexible, systematic approach to specific assignments and leaves a word trail so that instructors can help students confront problems during the exploration and planning of assignments and can reconstruct what went right and wrong after the paper is written. This classroom-tested form can save students and instructors time and effort, and produce effective results. A copy of the worksheet is located in the textbook on page 202, on the Student Companion Site, and on the Instructor Companion Site. It is discussed in the final two chapters. Instructors who require this sheet can ask their students to photocopy the generic version from the Student Companion Site or enlarge and copy it from their textbook. Instructors can also customize the Word copy on the Instructor Companion Site to fit their pedagogy or particular assignments.

⌒ Support Material for Instructors

- **Instructor's Guide for *At a Glance*.** The Instructor's Guide—available both in print at Cengage Learning, Higher Education, at 800-354-9706 and online at the Instructor's Companion Site—provides helpful hints for teaching *At a Glance* in the classroom. It includes sample syllabi; suggestions for working with basic writing students and ESL students; grading tips; Answer Keys; quizzes on sentence writing, handbook material, readings; and more.
- **Instructor Companion Site for *At a Glance*.** This instructor site presents helpful resources in addition to the Instructor's Guide, such as PowerPoint slides, at login.cengage.com.
- **Student Companion Site for *At a Glance* at www.cengagebrain .com.** The student site provides helpful resources such as sentence writing exercises, a 2009 MLA Guide and an APA Guide to documented papers, a printable Writing Process Worksheet, tips on writing resumes and letters of application, additional reading selections, and more.

⌒ Acknowledgments

I am profoundly indebted to the many instructors who have reviewed *At a Glance: Sentences* for these five editions and helped it grow and remain fresh and innovative. Here are a few of those thoughtful and imaginative reviewers: Cindi Clarke, Belmont Technical College; Tim Kelley, Northwest-Shoals Community College; Darin Cozzens, Surry Community College; James Crooks, Shasta College; Deborah Burson-Smith, Southern University at New Orleans; Karen A. Cahill, Southeastern Community College; Iris Gribble-Neal, Eastern Washington University; Ardyce Ketterling, Bismark State College; Tamara Kuzmankov, Tacoma Community College; David Lang, Golden Gate University; Lynette Lochasusen, Colorado Mountain College; Phyllis MacCameron, Erie Community

College; Kathy Masters, Arkansas State University; Sharon Owens, University of Texas at El Paso; Dianne Perkins, Community College of Philadelphia; John Richardson, Augusta Technical College; Judith Sinclair, Catholic University; Alice Steilder, Santa Barbara City College; Marilyn Strauss, Pace University; Steve Stremmel, American River College; Pamela A. Tackaburg, Fullerton College; David White, Walters State Community College; Marilyn Black, Middlesex Community College; Julie M. Kissel, Washtenaw Community College; Pat Leverentz, Pima Community College; Vern Lindquist, Sullivan County Community College; Laurel E. Spillum, Portland Community College; and Elin Tomov, Georgia Perimeter College.

I also deeply appreciate the expert, dedicated work of freelance principal editor Karen Mauk, production manager Nancy Benjamin with Books By Design, editorial specialist Ann Marie Radadiewicz, permissions editor Maria Leon Maimone, and my colleagues at Cengage Learning: Annie Todd, Kirsten Stoller, Katie Huha, Janine Tangney, Melanie Opacki, Ryan Ahern, Stacey Purviance, and Aimee Chevrette Bear.

I am especially grateful to my family for their cheerful, inspiring support: Sharon, Kelly, Erin, Michael, Kathy, Jessica, Deborah, Shane, Lauren, Jarrett, and Matthew.

Lee Brandon

Student Overview

This book is designed to help you write better sentences both separately and in context.

- In Chapters 1 through 6, you'll work with understanding sentence parts, identifying kinds of sentences, putting short sentences together to show relationships, fixing groups of words that look like sentences but really are not, and balancing the parts of a sentence.
- In Chapters 7 through 11, you'll study how to make the most effective use of verbs, pronouns, adjectives and adverbs, punctuation and capitalization, and spelling.
- In Chapter 12, you'll look at the writing process as a series of steps that can carry you from stage to stage until you have produced a polished paragraph or essay.
- In Chapter 13, you'll find instructions and more than one hundred topics for writing with specific and combined patterns of paragraphs and essays.

Following are some strategies to help you make the best use of this book and to jump-start the improvement in your writing skills.

1. **Be active and systematic in learning.** Take advantage of your instructor's expertise by being an active participant in class—one who takes notes, asks questions, and contributes to discussion. Become dedicated to systematic learning: determine your needs, decide what to do, and do it. Make learning a part of your everyday thinking and behavior.
2. **Read widely.** Samuel Johnson, a great English scholar, once said he didn't want to read anything by people who had written more than they had read. William Faulkner, a Nobel Prize winner in literature, said, "Read, read, read. Read everything—trash, classics, good and bad, and see how writers do it." Read to learn technique, to acquire ideas, to be stimulated to write. Especially read to satisfy your curiosity and receive pleasure. If reading is a main component of your course, approach it as systematically as you do writing.

3. **Keep a journal.** Keeping a journal may not be required in your particular class, but, required or not, jotting down your observations in a notebook is a good idea. Here are some ideas for daily, or almost daily, journal writing:

- Summarize, evaluate, or react to reading assignments.
- Summarize, evaluate, or react to what you see on television and in movies, and to what you read in newspapers and magazines.
- Describe and narrate situations or events you experience.
- Write about career-related matters you encounter in other courses or on the job.

   Your journal entries may read like an intellectual diary, a record of what you are thinking about at certain times. Keeping a journal will help you to understand reading material better, to develop more language skills, and to think more clearly—as well as to become more confident and write more easily so that writing becomes a comfortable everyday activity. It is important to get into the habit of writing something each day.

4. **Evaluate your writing skills.** Use the Self-Evaluation Chart inside the front cover of this book to list areas you need to work on. You can add to your lists throughout the entire term. Drawing on your instructor's comments, make notes on matters such as spelling, word choice, paragraph development, grammar, sentences, punctuation, and capitalization. As you master each problem area, you can check it off or cross it out.

   Here is a partially completed Self-Evaluation Chart, followed by some guidelines for filling out your own.

Self-Evaluation Chart

Spelling/ Word Choice	Paragraph Development	Grammar/ Sentences	Punctuation/ Capitalization

receive 180
a lot 186
its, it's 171
could of,
   could have
   186
	topic
	   sentence 195
	support 198
		fragment 59
		variety of
		   patterns 29
		comma
		   splice 67
		run-on 67
			apostrophe 171
			comma 153
			semicolon 160
			question mark
			   with
			   quotation
			   marks 153

- *Spelling/Word Choice.* List words marked as incorrectly spelled on your assignments. Master the words on your list and add new words as you accumulate assignments. Also include new, useful words with their brief definitions and comments on word choice, such as avoiding slang, clichés, and vague or general words.
- *Paragraph Development.* List suggestions your instructor made about writing strong topic sentences and attending to matters such as coherence, unity, emphasis, language, support, and sentences.
- *Grammar/Sentences.* As you go through this book, if you find that you did not completely master a section, list here any special problems you have before moving to the next section. Also, list comments from your instructor.
- *Punctuation/Capitalization.* List any problems you encounter with punctuation and capitalization. Because the items in this column may be covered in Chapter 10, you can often use both rule numbers and page numbers for the references here.

5. **Take full advantage of the *At a Glance* Student Companion Site at www.cengagebrain.com and other technology.** Using a computer will enable you to write, revise, and edit more swiftly as you move, alter, check, and delete material with a few keystrokes. The Student Companion Site offers additional exercises and instruction. Many colleges have writing labs with good instruction and facilities for networking and researching complicated topics. The Internet, used wisely, can provide resource material for compositions.

6. **Use the Writing Process Worksheet.** Record details about each of your assignments, such as the due date, topic, length, and form. The worksheet will also remind you of the stages of the writing process: explore, organize, and write. A blank Writing Process Worksheet for you to enlarge and photocopy for assignments appears on page 202, and a printable copy is on the Student Companion Site.

7. **Be positive.** All the elements you record in your Self-Evaluation Chart probably are covered in *At a Glance: Sentences*. The table of contents, the index, and the correction chart on the inside back cover of the book will direct you to the additional instruction you decide you need. Soon, seeing what you have mastered and checked off your list will give you a sense of accomplishment.

Finally, don't compare yourself with others. Compare yourself with yourself and, as you make progress, consider yourself what you are—a student on the path toward effective writing, a student on the path toward success.

1

Parts of Speech

Why does this book begin with parts of speech? The answer is twofold:

- First, the parts of speech are the most basic word units you will work with in this book. Here at the outset you will learn, or review, how parts of speech function in communicating ideas, and what you can and cannot do effectively with each one in your writing. Knowing parts of speech is one of your gateways to experimenting with confidence in writing. Your understanding of them will be reinforced in each of the following chapters.
- Second, knowing the names of the parts of speech will allow you to discuss the language you use and will help you understand your instructors' comments on writing, specifically on your writing. This principle can be applied to all areas of learning. Knowing terminology enables you to communicate with others. In discussing computers, for example, without knowing basic terminology—*mouse, booting up, desktop, Internet Explorer, user name, gigabyte*—you would be tongue-tied when you were trying to learn or needed technical help. The same goes for you as a student of writing. By the time you have finished this book, you will know parts of speech well.

To classify a word as a part of speech, we observe two simple principles:

1. The word must be in the context of communication, usually in a sentence. The first principle is important because some words can be any of several parts of speech. The word *round*, for example, can function as five:
    - I watched the potter *round* the block of clay. (verb)
    - I saw her go *round* the corner. (preposition)
    - She has a *round* head. (adjective)

1

- The astronauts watched the world go *round*. (adverb)
- The champ knocked him out in one *round*. (noun)

2. We must be able to identify the word with other parts of speech that have similar characteristics: nouns, pronouns, verbs, adjectives, adverbs, prepositions, conjunctions, or interjections.

~/ Nouns

Nouns are naming words. Nouns may name persons, animals, plants, places, things, substances, qualities, or ideas—for example, *Bart, armadillo, Mayberry, tree, rock, cloud, love, ghost, music,* and *virtue.*

Nouns are often pointed out by noun indicators. These noun indicators—*the, a, an*—signal that a noun is ahead, although there may be words between the indicator and the noun itself.

the slime	*a* werewolf	*an* aardvark
the green slime	*a* hungry werewolf	*an* angry aardvark

~/ Pronouns

A **pronoun** is a word that is used in place of a noun.

- Some pronouns may represent specific persons or things:

I	she	they	you
me	her	them	yourself
myself	herself	themselves	yourselves
it	he	we	who
itself	him	us	whom
that	himself	ourselves	

- Indefinite pronouns refer to nouns (persons, places, things) in a general way:

each	everyone	nobody	somebody

- Other pronouns point out particular things:

SINGULAR *this, that*	PLURAL *these, those*
This is my treasure.	*These* are my jewels.
That is your junk.	*Those* are your trinkets.

- Still other pronouns introduce questions.

    Which is the best CD player?

    What are the main ingredients of a Twinkie?

∿ Verbs

Verbs show action or express being in relation to the subject of a sentence. They customarily occur in set positions in sentences.

- **Action verbs** are usually easy to identify.

    The aardvark *ate* the crisp, tasty ants. (action verb)

    The aardvark *washed* them down with a snoutful of water. (action verb)

- The *being* verbs are few in number and are also easy to identify. The most common *being* verbs are *is, was, were, are,* and *am.*

    Harry Potter lives in a fictional universe. (*being* verb)

    I *am* his enthusiastic fan. (*being* verb)

- The form of a verb expresses its tense, that is, the time of the action or being. The time may be in the present or past.

    Bruce Springsteen *sings* "Born to Run." (present)

    Bruce Springsteen *sang* "Born to Run." (past)

- One or more **helping verbs** may be used with the main verb to form other tenses. The combination is called a **verb phrase.**

    He *has sung* the song many times for huge crowds in stadiums. (Helping verb and main verb indicate a time in the past.)

    He *will be singing* the song many more times while on tours. (Helping verbs and main verb indicate a time in the future.)

- Some helping verbs can be used alone as main verbs: *has, have, had, is, was, were, are,* and *am.* Certain other helping verbs function only as helpers: *will, shall, should,* and *could.*

    The most common position for the verb is directly after the subject or after the subject and its modifiers.

    At high noon only two men [subject] *were* on Main Street.

    The man with the faster draw [subject and modifiers] *walked* away alone.

〜 Adjectives

Adjectives modify nouns and pronouns. Most adjectives answer the questions *What kind? Which one?* and *How many?*

- Adjectives answering the *What kind?* question are descriptive. They tell the quality, kind, or condition of the nouns or pronouns they modify.

red convertible	*dirty* fork
noisy muffler	*wild* roses
The rain is *gentle.*	Bob was *tired.*

- Adjectives answering the *Which one?* question narrow or restrict the meaning of a noun. Some of these are pronouns that become adjectives by function.

my money	*our* ideas	the *other* house
this reason	*these* apples	

- Adjectives answering the *How many?* question are, of course, numbering words.

some people	*each* pet	*few* goals
three dollars	*one* glove	

- The words *a, an,* and *the* are adjectives called **articles.** As "noun indicators," they point out persons, places, and things.

〜 Adverbs

Adverbs modify (describe or explain) verbs, adjectives, and other adverbs. Adverbs answer the questions *How? Where? When?* and *To what degree?*

MODIFYING VERBS   They <u>did</u> their work <u>quickly.</u>
                         v   adv

                     He <u>replied</u> <u>angrily.</u>
                         v   adv

MODIFYING ADJECTIVES   They were <u>somewhat</u> <u>happy.</u>
                                   adv   adj

MODIFYING ADVERBS   She answered <u>very slowly.</u>
                                 adv   adv

- Adverbs that answer the *How?* question are concerned with manner or way.

    Irena ate the burgers *hungrily*.   Moe snored *noisily*.

- Adverbs that answer the *Where?* question show location.

    They drove *downtown*.   Loretta climbed *upstairs*.
    Joseph stayed *behind*.

- Adverbs that answer the *When?* question indicate time.

    The ship sailed *yesterday*.   I expect an answer *soon*.

- Adverbs that answer the *To what degree?* question express extent.

    Barbara is *entirely* correct.   Pete was *somewhat* annoyed.

Most words ending in -*ly* are adverbs.

    Ramon completed the task skillfully.
    <u>   adv</u>

    Silvia answered him courteously.
    <u>   adv</u>

However, there are a few exceptions.

    The house provided a lovely view of the valley.
    <u>   adj</u>

    Your intimidation mask is creepy.
    <u>   adj</u>

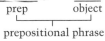 Prepositions

A **preposition** is a word or group of words that function as a connective. The preposition connects its object(s) to some other word(s) in the sentence. A preposition and its object(s)—usually a noun or pronoun—with modifiers make up a **prepositional phrase**.

    Bart worked against great odds.
            prep   object
            └───────┬───────┘
          prepositional phrase

    Everyone in his household cheered his effort.
            prep   object
            └───────┬───────┘
          prepositional phrase

Following are some of the most common prepositions:

about	before	but	into	past
above	behind	by	like	to
across	below	despite	near	toward
after	beneath	down	of	under
against	beside	for	off	until
among	between	from	on	upon
around	beyond	in	over	with

Some prepositions are composed of more than one word and are formed from other parts of speech:

according to	as far as	because of	in spite of
ahead of	as well as	in back of	instead of
along with	aside from	in front of	together with

A prepositional phrase can serve as an adjective or adverb within the sentence structure.

The car <u>with</u> the <u>dent</u> is mine.
       prep   object
prepositional phrase modifying *car*, a noun
adjective

A storm is forming <u>on</u> the <u>horizon</u>.
       prep   object
prepositional phrase modifying *is forming*, a verb phrase
adverb

Caution: Do not confuse adverbs with prepositions

I went *across* slowly. (without an object—adverb)

I went *across* the field. (with an object—preposition)

We walked *behind* silently. (without an object—adverb)

We walked *behind* the mall. (with an object—preposition)

～ Conjunctions

A **conjunction** connects and shows a relationship between words, phrases, or clauses. A phrase is two or more words acting as a part of speech. A clause is a group of words with a subject and a verb. An independent clause can stand by itself: *Jolene plays bass guitar.* A dependent clause cannot stand by itself: *when Jolene plays bass guitar.*

The two kinds of conjunctions are coordinating and subordinating.

Coordinating conjunctions connect words, phrases, and clauses of equal rank: noun with noun, adjective with adjective, verb with verb, phrase with phrase, main clause with main clause, and subordinate clause with subordinate clause. The seven common coordinating conjunctions are *for, and, nor, but, or, yet,* and *so.* (An easy way to remember them is to think of the acronym FANBOYS, which is made up of the first letter of each conjunction.)

TWO NOUNS   Bring a <u>pencil</u> <u>and</u> some <u>paper</u>.
                        noun conj   noun

TWO PHRASES   Did she go <u>to the store</u> <u>or</u> <u>to the game</u>?
                              prep phrase conj prep phrase

Paired conjunctions such as *either/or, neither/nor,* or *both/and* are usually classed as coordinating conjunctions.

<u>Neither</u> the coach <u>nor</u> the manager was at fault.
  conj   conj

Subordinating conjunctions connect dependent clauses with main clauses. Here is a list of the most common subordinating conjunctions:

after	because	provided	whenever
although	before	since	where
as	but that	so that	whereas
as if	if	till	wherever
as long as	in order that	until	
as soon as	notwithstanding	when	

If the dependent clause comes *before* the main clause, it is set off by a comma.

<u>Although</u> <u>she</u> <u>was</u> in pain, she stayed in the game.
  conj   subj   v
  └────┬────┘
  dependent clause

If the dependent clause comes *after* the main clause, it usually is *not* set off by a comma.

She stayed in the game <u>because</u> <u>she</u> <u>was needed</u>.
                          conj   subj   v
                          └─────┬─────┘
                          dependent clause

Caution: Certain words can function as either conjunctions or prepositions. It is necessary to look ahead to see if the word introduces a clause with a subject and verb—conjunction function—or takes an object—preposition function. Some of the words with two functions are *after, for, since,* and *until.*

> *After* the concert was over, we went home. (clause follows—conjunction)
>
> *After* the concert, we went home. (object follows—preposition)

Interjections

An **interjection** conveys strong emotion or surprise. When an interjection appears alone, it is usually punctuated with an exclamation mark. An interjection can be more than one word, and almost any word or phrase can be an interjection if it is to be charged with feeling.

> Right! Wow! Yikes! Duh! Cowabunga! Yoink! Woo-hoo!

When it appears as part of a sentence, an interjection is usually followed by a comma.

> Oh, I did not consider that problem.

The interjection may sound exciting, but it is seldom appropriate for college writing.

Chapter Review

Exercise 1 Identifying Parts of Speech

Indicate the part of speech of each italicized word or group of words by placing the appropriate abbreviations in the blanks.

n	noun	pro	pronoun
v	verb	adj	adjective
adv	adverb	conj	conjunction
prep	preposition		

_____ _____ 1. *For* about forty years, the Three Stooges were a popular *comedy* team.

_____ _____ 2. They were *often* accused of making films *in* bad taste, but no one accused them of being good actors.

_____   _____   3. For decades they *made seven* or more pictures a year.

_____   _____   4. Actually six *different* actors *played* the parts.

_____   _____   5. The *most* famous threesome *was* Moe, Curly, and Larry.

_____   _____   6. The Stooges specialized *in physical* comedy.

_____   _____   7. They *took* special *delight* in hitting each other in the head and poking each other's eyes.

_____   _____   8. Moe was the on-screen *leader* of this *zany* group.

_____   _____   9. He assumed leadership in each film *because he* was more intelligent than the others, which isn't saying much.

_____   _____   10. Curly was not bright, but he made up for his *dumbness* by having the *hardest* head in the world, at least in the world of Stooge movies.

_____   _____   11. Larry *often got caught* between the flailing arms and kicking feet of Moe and Curly.

_____   _____   12. The movies made *by* the Stooges *usually* came in two reels and were shown along with feature-length films.

_____   _____   13. The Stooge movies *were given* such *titles* as *Half-Wits*, *Three Hams on Rye*, *Slap Happy Sleuths*, and *Matri Phony*.

_____   _____   14. They made fun of *dignity* and physically abused each other with all kinds *of* lethal instruments, but they never got hurt.

_____   _____   15. They received *little respect* from the film-making community.

_____   _____   16. Only Moe saved *his* money *and* became wealthy.

_____   _____   17. Apparently Curly *at* times lived his *movie* role off stage.

_____   _____   18. After a *brief* marriage, Curly's wife *left* him, saying he punched, poked, pinched, and pushed her and left cigar butts in the sink.

_____   _____   19. Moe tried to gain *respectability* as a character actor, but the audiences could never accept *him* in serious roles.

_____   _____   20. A whole new television *audience has made* the Three Stooges the stars they never were in their lifetimes.

Exercise 2   Identifying Parts of Speech

Indicate the part of speech of each italicized word or group of words by placing the appropriate abbreviations in the blanks.

n	noun	pro	pronoun
v	verb	adj	adjective
adv	adverb	conj	conjunction
prep	preposition		

_____   _____   1. The *turtle* can be defined as a reptile *with* a shell.

_____   _____   2. It is a *toothless* creature that can *smell* and see well.

_____   _____   3. Some live *mostly* in the water, whereas others live mostly *in* places as dry as the desert.

_____   _____   4. Both sea *and land* turtles will burrow and hibernate.

_____   _____   5. Turtles are well known *for their* longevity.

_____   _____   6. *Some live* to be more than a hundred years old.

_____   _____   7. *Many* people purchase turtles for *pets*.

_____   _____   8. Young turtles *eat chopped* raw meat, greens, fish, and worms.

_____   _____   9. *They* need both sunlight *and* shade.

_____ _____ 10. *Some* people paint their *pet* turtles, a practice that can damage the turtles' shells.

_____ _____ 11. *Most* turtles are not *suitable* for pets.

_____ _____ 12. The snapping turtle *is* one such *species*.

_____ _____ 13. *It* can be *vicious* when cornered.

_____ _____ 14. The *common* snapper weighs up to sixty pounds and can snap off a set of fingers *with* one bite.

_____ _____ 15. Folklore holds that *when* a snapping turtle bites someone, it will not let go *until* it hears thunder.

_____ _____ 16. Stories *circulate* about a farmer who cut off the head of a snapping turtle that was biting someone, *yet,* even without its body, the snapper would not let go.

_____ _____ 17. The box turtle is a *gentle creature* and makes a good pet.

_____ _____ 18. It has a *hooked* beak, red eyes, and a splotchy *yellow* and brown shell.

_____ _____ 19. It eats worms, snails, berries, *and* other *fruit.*

_____ _____ 20. In the summer in the Midwest, one can *find* many box turtles crawling about, their solemn beaks red from a *meal* of blackberries.

2

Subjects and Verbs

The two crucial parts of any sentence are the subject and the verb.

- The **subject** is who or what causes the action or expresses a state of being.
- The **verb** indicates what the subject is doing or is being.

The subject and verb often carry the meaning of the sentence. Consider this example:

> The <u>woman</u> <u>left</u> for work.
> subject   verb

The subject *woman* and the verb *left* indicate the basic content of the sentence while providing structure. So important are the subject and the verb that they alone are sufficient to create a complete sentence.

> Jacob runs.
> Grace thinks.

Subjects

The **simple subject** of a sentence is usually a single noun or pronoun.

> The judge's <u>reputation</u> for order in the courtroom is well known.
> simple subject

The **complete subject** is the simple subject with all its modifiers—that is, with all the words that describe or qualify it.

> <u>The judge's reputation for order in the courtroom</u> is well known.
> complete subject

To more easily identify simple subjects of sentences, you may want to review the following information about nouns and pronouns. (You may also review Chapter 1, "Parts of Speech.")

Nouns

Nouns are naming words. Nouns may name persons, animals, plants, places, things, substances, qualities, or ideas—for example, *Manny, armadillo, Atlanta, tree, rock, cloud, love, ghost, music,* and *virtue.*

Pronouns

A **pronoun** is a word that is used in place of a noun.

- Pronouns that can be used as subjects of sentences may represent specific persons or things and are called personal pronouns:

I	we
you	you
he, she, it	they

  EXAMPLE   <u>They</u> recommended my sister for the coaching position.
         subject

- Indefinite pronouns refer to nouns (persons, places, things) in a general way:

each	everyone	nobody	somebody
either	neither	anyone	someone

  EXAMPLE   <u>Everyone</u> wants a copy of that photograph.
         subject

- Other pronouns point out particular things:

  SINGULAR *this, that*   PLURAL *these, those*

  This is my treasure.   *These* are my jewels.

  That is your junk.   *Those* are your trinkets.

- Still other pronouns introduce questions:

  Which is the best CD player?

  What are the main ingredients in a Twinkie?

  Who understands this computer command?

Caution: To be the subject of a sentence, a pronoun must stand alone.

  This is a treasure. (Subject is *this;* pronoun stands alone.)

  This *treasure* is mine. (Subject is *treasure. This* is an adjective—a word that describes a noun; *this* describes *treasure.*)

Compound Subjects

A subject may be **compound**. That is, it may consist of two or more subjects, usually joined by *and* or *or*, that function together.

> The *prosecutor* and the *attorney* for the defense made opening statements.
>
> *Luke* and his *friends* listened carefully.

Implied Subjects

A subject may be **implied** or understood. An imperative sentence—a sentence that gives a command—has *you* as the implied subject.

> (You) Sit in that chair, please.
>
> (You) Now take the oath.
>
> (You) Please read the notes carefully.

Trouble Spots

A **prepositional phrase** starts with a preposition (a word such as *at, in, of, to,* or *with*) and ends with one or more nouns or pronouns with their modifiers: *at the time, by the jury, in the courtroom, to the judge and the media, with controlled anger.* Some of the most common prepositions are the following:

about	before	but	into	past
above	behind	by	like	to
across	below	despite	near	toward
after	beneath	down	of	under
against	beside	for	off	until
among	between	from	on	upon
around	beyond	in	over	with

Some prepositions are composed of more than one word and are formed from other parts of speech:

according to	as far as	because of	in spite of
ahead of	as well as	in back of	instead of
along with	aside from	in front of	together with

Be careful not to confuse the subject of a sentence with the noun or pronoun (known as the **object of the preposition**) in a prepositional phrase. The object of a preposition (the final noun or pronoun of a prepositional phrase) cannot be the subject of a sentence.

The car with the dents is mine.
subject/prepositional phrase

The subject of the sentence is *car*. The word *dents* is the object of the preposition *with* and cannot be the subject of the sentence.

Most of the pie has been eaten.
subject/prepositional phrase

The person in the middle of the crowd has disappeared.
subject/prepositional phrase/prepositional phrase

The words *there* and *here* are adverbs (or filler words) and cannot be subjects.

There is no problem.
subject

Here is the issue.
subject

Exercise 1 Finding Subjects

Underline the simple or the compound subject, without modifiers.

EXAMPLE   A highly developed social structure and the use of
bronze were marks of the Shang dynasty (about 1766 to
1122 BCE).

1. The earliest evidence of Chinese writing comes from that

   dynasty.

2. Archaeologists have found hundreds of animal bones and shells.

3. The bones and shells have written symbols on them.

4. These objects with writing on them are known as oracle bones.

5. Priests told fortunes with them.

6. Part of today's Chinese culture was developed 3,500 years ago.

7. In the Chinese method of writing, each character stands for an

   idea, not for a sound.

8. Some of the characters are very much like those in a modern Chinese newspaper.

9. They are not like Egyptian hieroglyphs.

10. Those Egyptian symbols stood for sounds in the spoken language.

11. In the Chinese language, there are practically no links between written and spoken forms.

12. Study your Chinese 101 textbook for more insights.

Exercise 2 Finding Subjects

Underline the simple or the compound subject, without modifiers.

1. Mahatma Gandhi gave his life for India and for peace.

2. Through a practice of nonviolent resistance, he led his people to freedom from the British.

3. Ponder his preference for behavior rather than accomplishment.

4. There was only good in his behavior and in his accomplishments.

5. His fasts, writings, and speeches inspired the people of India.

6. He taught his people self-sufficiency in weaving cloth and making salt for themselves against British law.

7. Gandhi urged the tolerance of all religions.

8. Finally, the British granted freedom to India.

9. Some leaders in India and a few foreign agitators questioned

the freedom of religion.

10. Gandhi, the Indian prince of peace, was killed by an intolerant

religious leader.

 Verbs

Verbs show action or express being in relation to the subject of a sentence.

Types of Verbs

Action verbs show movement or accomplishment of an idea or a deed. Someone can *"consider* the statement" or *"hit* the ball." Here are other examples:

> Molina *left* the arena.
> Yuma *bought* the book.
> They *adopted* the child.
> Tao *understood* her main theories.

Being verbs indicate existence. Few in number, they include *is, was, were, am,* and *are.*

> The movie *is* sad.
> The book *was* comprehensive.
> They *were* responsible.
> I *am* concerned.
> We *are* organized.

Verb Phrases

Verbs may occur as single words or as phrases. A **verb phrase** is made up of a main verb and one or more helping verbs such as the following:

is	was	can	have
are	were	could	had
am	will	would	has

Here are some sentences that contain verb phrases:

The judge *has presided* over many capital cases.

His rulings *are* seldom *overturned* on appeal.

I *should have known* the answer.

Compound Verbs

Verbs that are joined by a word such as *and* or *or* are called **compound verbs**.

The prosecutor *had presented* and *had won* famous cases.

Karla *prepared* carefully and *presented* her ideas with clarity.

We *will go* out for dinner or *skip* it entirely.

Compound verbs show two physical or mental actions performed by a simple or a compound subject.

Verbals

Do not confuse verbs with verbals. **Verbals** are verblike words in certain respects, but they function as other parts of speech. The three kinds of verbals are infinitives, gerunds, and participles.

An **infinitive** is made up of the word *to* and a verb. An infinitive provides information, but, unlike the true verb, it is not tied to the subject of the sentence. It acts as a noun or describing unit.

He wanted *to get* a bachelor's degree. (As an object of the verb *wanted*, *to get* acts as a noun and is an infinitive.)

A bachelor's degree is not easy *to obtain*. (As a modifier, or describer, of *easy*, *to obtain* acts as an adverb and is an infinitive.)

A **gerund** is a verblike word ending in -*ing* that acts as a noun.

Going to work was her main objective. (the activity of going to work)

She thought about *going* to work. (the act of going)

Going in each sentence acts as a noun. In the first sentence, it is the subject of the sentence. In the second, it is the object of the preposition *about*.

A **participle** is a verblike word that usually has an -*ing* or an -*ed* ending.

Walking to town in the dark, Luther lost his way.

Wanted by the FBI, Rachel was on the run.

In the first example, the word *walking* answers the question *When?* In the second, the word *wanted* answers the question *Which one?* Both *walking* and *wanted* are describing words; they are not the true verbs in the sentences.

Caution: Do not confuse verbals with true verbs. Verbals serve as nouns or modifiers. *Never, not,* and *hardly* are also modifiers, not verbs.

The attorney could *not* win the case without key witnesses. (*Not* is an adverb. The verb phrase is *could win.*)

The jury could *hardly* hear the witness. (*Hardly* is an adverb; *could hear* is the verb phrase.)

Exercise 3 Finding Verbs

Underline the verb(s) in each sentence.

1. Chimpanzees live and travel in social groups.

2. The composition of these groups varies in age and gender.

3. The habitat of the chimpanzees is mainly forests.

4. They spend more time in the trees than on the ground.

5. Each night they make a nest of branches and leaves in trees.

6. Sometimes a proud male will beat on his chest.

7. Chimpanzees are violent at times but usually live peacefully.

8. After finding food, a chimp hoots and shakes branches.

9. Other chimps hear the commotion and go to the food source.

10. Chimp tools, such as leaf sponges and sticks, are primitive.

Exercise 4 Finding Verbs

Underline the verb(s) in each sentence.

1. Chimpanzees share many features with human beings.

2. More than 90 percent of basic genetic make-up is shared.

3. Both human beings and chimps can use reason.

4. Chimps have a remarkable talent for communication.

5. Chimps do not have the capacity for human speech.

6. However, chimps can use other symbols.

7. In one experiment, chimps learned American Sign Language.

8. Chimps can learn a complex system of language.

9. Chimp scholar Washoe learned more than 160 signs and could

   ask questions.

10. Another chimp, Lana, uses a computer.

Exercise 5 Finding Subjects and Verbs

Circle the subject(s) and underline the verb(s) in the following sentences. You will have to supply the subject for one sentence.

1. Read this exercise carefully.

2. What causes earthquakes?

3. How much damage can they do?

4. Earthquakes shake the earth.

5. There is no simple answer to the question of cause.

6. The earth is covered by rock plates.

7. Instead of merely covering, they are in constant motion.

8. These plates bump into each other and then pass over each other.

9. The rocks are squeezed and stretched.

10. They pull apart or pile up and cause breaks in the earth's surface.

11. These breaks are called *faults*.

12. The formation of a fault is an earthquake.

13. During the breaking or shifting, a seismic wave travels across the earth's surface.

14. These quaking vibrations are especially destructive near the point of the breaking or shifting.

15. Their force is equal to as much as ten thousand times that of an atomic bomb.

16. For many years, scientists have tried to predict earthquakes.

17. There has been little success in their endeavors.

18. Earthquakes are identified only after the fact.

19. Some states, such as California, experience many earthquakes.

20. Somewhere in the earth, a quake of some magnitude is almost certainly occurring now.

～ Location of Subjects and Verbs

Although the subject *usually* appears before the verb, it may follow the verb instead:

Into the court <u>stumbled</u> the <u>defendant</u>.
                         verb   subject

From tiny acorns <u>grow</u> mighty <u>oaks</u>.
                    verb   subject

There <u>was</u> little <u>support</u> for him in the audience.
      verb   subject

Here <u>are</u> your <u>books</u> and your <u>papers</u>.
    verb   subject   subject

Verb phrases are often broken up in a question. Do not overlook a part of the verb that is separated from another in a question such as "Where had the defendant gone on that fateful night?" If you have trouble finding the verb phrase, recast the question, making it into a statement: "The defendant *had gone* where on that fateful night." The result will not necessarily be a smooth or complete statement, but you will be able to see the basic elements more easily.

Can the defense lawyer control the direction of the trial?

Change the question to a statement to find the verb phrase:

The defense lawyer *can control* the direction of the trial.

～ Chapter Review

Exercise 6 Finding Subjects and Verbs

Circle the subject(s) and underline the verb(s) in the following sentences. You will have to supply the subject for one sentence.

1. Consider this information about Puerto Rico.

2. Just where is Puerto Rico?

3. What do the words *Puerto Rico* mean?

4. Are Puerto Ricans U.S. citizens?

5. How is Puerto Rico different from our states?

6. Will it ever become a state?

7. The Commonwealth of Puerto Rico is located southeast

   of Florida.

8. *Puerto Rico* means "rich port."

9. Puerto Rico became a U.S. territory in 1898 after the Spanish-

   American War.

10. It became a commonwealth with its own constitution in 1952.

11. Puerto Ricans are citizens of the United States.

12. They cannot vote in presidential elections and do not pay

    federal income taxes.

13. On several occasions, they have voted not to become a state.

14. However, there are many in favor of statehood.

15. The majority of the citizens speak Spanish.

16. Their economy is based on manufacturing, fishing, and agriculture.

17. The Caribbean National Forest is treasured by Puerto Ricans

    and visitors.

18. In this tropical rain forest, parrots and orchids can be seen.

19. Tourists by the thousands visit the Phosphorescent Bay at

    La Parguera.

20. On moonless nights, the phosphorescent plankton light the water.

Exercise 7 Finding Subjects and Verbs

Circle the simple or the compound subject(s) and underline the verb(s) in the following sentences. You will have to supply the subject for one sentence.

1. Read this exercise and learn about the Aztec empire in Mexico.

2. Aztec cities were as large as those in Europe at that time.

3. Government and religion were important concerns.

4. There was little difference between the two institutions.

5. They built huge temples to their gods and sacrificed human beings.

6. The religious ceremonies related mainly to their concerns about plentiful harvests.

7. Aztec society had nobles, commoners, serfs, and slaves.

8. The family included a husband, a wife, children, and some relatives of the husband.

9. At the age of ten, boys went to school and girls either went to school or learned domestic skills at home.

10. The Aztecs wore loose-fitting garments, they lived in adobe houses, and they ate tortillas.

11. Scholars in this culture developed a calendar of 365 days.

12. Huge Aztec calendars of stone are now in museums.

13. The Aztec language was similar to that of the Comanche and Pima Indians.

14. The Aztec written language was pictographic and represented ideas and sounds.

15. Both religion and government required young men to pursue warfare.

16. By pursuing warfare, the soldiers could capture others for slaves and sacrifice, and they could enlarge the Aztec empire.

17. In 1519, Hernando Cortez landed in Mexico.

18. He was joined by native people other than Aztecs.

19. After first welcoming Cortez and his army, the Aztecs then rebelled.

20. The Spaniards killed Emperor Montezuma II, and then they defeated the Aztecs.

Exercise 8 Writing Sentences with Subjects and Verbs

Using the topic of work, *write five sentences. Circle the simple or the compound subject(s) and underline the verb(s).*

1. _____

_____

_____

_____

_____

2. _____

_____

_____

_____

_____

3. _____

_____

_____

_____

_____

4. _____

_____

_____

_____

_____

5. _____

_____

_____

_____

_____

3

Kinds of Sentences

The four kinds of basic sentences in English are simple, compound, complex, and compound-complex. The terms may be new to you, but if you can recognize subjects and verbs, with a little instruction and practice you should be able to identify and write any of the four kinds of sentences. The only new idea to master is the concept of the *clause*.

~ Clauses

A **clause** is a group of words with a subject and a verb that functions as a part or all of a complete sentence. There are two kinds of clauses: independent (main) and dependent (subordinate).

> INDEPENDENT CLAUSE   I have the money.
>
> DEPENDENT CLAUSE   When I have the money

Independent Clauses

An **independent (main) clause** is a group of words with a subject and a verb that can stand alone and make sense. An independent clause expresses a complete thought by itself and can be written as a separate sentence.

> Avita plays the bass guitar.
>
> The manager is not at fault.

Dependent Clauses

A **dependent clause** is a group of words with a subject and a verb that depends on a main clause to give it meaning.

> since Helen came home (no meaning alone)
>
> <u>Since Helen came home,</u> <u>her mother has been happy.</u> (has meaning)
>   dependent clause   independent clause

27

because she was needed (no meaning alone)

She stayed in the game because she was needed. (has meaning)

      independent clause   dependent clause

Dependent clauses are connected to the rest of the sentence by subordinating conjunctions such as the following:

after	if	until
although	in order that	when
as	provided that	whenever
as if	rather than	where
because	since	whereas
before	so that	wherever
even if	than	whether
even though	unless	while

Relative Clauses

A **relative clause,** one type of dependent clause, begins with a relative pronoun, a pronoun such as *that, which,* or *who.* Relative pronouns *relate* the clause to another word in the sentence.

that fell last night (no meaning alone)

The snow that fell last night is nearly gone. (has meaning)

          dependent clause

In the sentence above, the relative pronoun *that* relates the dependent clause to the subject of the sentence, *snow.*

who stayed in the game (no meaning alone)

She was the only one who stayed in the game.

    independent clause   dependent clause

In the sentence above, the relative pronoun *who* relates the dependent clause to the word *one.*

Trouble Spot: Phrases

A **phrase** is a group of words that go together. It differs from a clause in that a phrase does not have a subject and a verb. So far, we have seen prepositional phrases (*in the house, beyond the horizon*) and verbal phrases (infinitive phrase: *to go home;* participial phrase: *disconnected from the printer;* and gerund phrase: *running the computer*).

Exercise 1 Identifying Clauses and Phrases

Identify the following groups of words as an independent, or a main, clause (has a subject and verb and can stand alone); a dependent clause (has a subject and verb but cannot stand alone); or a phrase (a group of words that go together but do not have a subject and a verb).

_____ 1. Under the table

_____ 2. After I won the lottery

_____ 3. I won the lottery

_____ 4. To find a fossil

_____ 5. Fred found a fossil

_____ 6. Over the bridge and through the woods

_____ 7. We chased the wind over the bridge and through the woods

_____ 8. Because it rated highly

_____ 9. Find matching socks

_____ 10. Because of the new guidelines

◠ Types of Sentences

The following discussion covers sentence types according to this principle: On the basis of the number and kinds of clauses it contains, a sentence may be classified as simple, compound, complex, or compound-complex.

Type	Definition	Example
Simple	One independent clause	She did the work well.
Compound	Two or more independent clauses	She did the work well, and she was paid well.
Complex	One independent clause (underlined) and one or more dependent clauses (italicized)	*Because she did the work well,* she was paid well.
Compound-Complex	Two or more independent clauses and one or more dependent clauses	*Because she did the work well,* she was paid well, and she was satisfied.

Simple Sentences

A **simple sentence** consists of one independent clause and no dependent clauses. It may contain phrases and have more than one subject or verb.

> The *lake looks* beautiful in the moonlight. (one subject and one verb)
>
> The *Army, Navy,* and *Marines sent* troops to the disaster area. (three subjects and one verb)
>
> *We sang* the old songs and *danced* happily at their wedding. (one subject and two verbs)
>
> My *father, mother,* and *sister came* to the school play, *applauded* the performers, and *attended* the party afterward. (three subjects and three verbs)

Exercise 2 Writing Simple Sentences

Write six simple sentences. The first five have been started for you.

1. This school _____

   _____

2. My desk _____

   _____

3. My friend _____

   _____

4. In the evening, I _____

   _____

5. Last night, the _____

   _____

6. _____

   _____

Compound Sentences

A **compound sentence** consists of two or more independent clauses with no dependent clauses. Take, for example, the following two independent clauses:

He opened the door. He found the missing paper.

Here are three ways to join the independent clauses to form a compound sentence.

1. Connect the two independent clauses using a connecting word called a **coordinating conjunction.** The coordinating conjunctions are *for, and, nor, but, or, yet, so*. Remember the acronym FANBOYS.

   He opened the door, *and* he found the missing paper.

   He opened the door, *so* he found the missing paper.

   Use a comma before the coordinating conjunction between two independent clauses (unless one of the clauses is extremely short).

2. Put a semicolon between the clauses.

   He opened the door; he found the missing paper.

3. Use a transitional word, such as *however* or *therefore*. Place a semicolon before the word and a comma after.

   He found the missing paper; *therefore,* he was satisfied.

Exercise 3 Writing Compound Sentences

Write five compound sentences using coordinating conjunctions. The sentences have been started for you. Then write the same five compound sentences without the coordinating conjunctions. Use a semicolon to join the independent clauses, and, if appropriate, include transitional words such as therefore *and* however.

1. He played well in the first quarter, but he _____

   _____

2. She was happy for a while, and then _____

   _____

3. The dog is our best friend, for _____

_____

4. She is not the best player, nor is _____

_____

5. I will try to help, but _____

_____

6. _____

_____

7. _____

_____

8. _____

_____

9. _____

_____

10. _____

_____

Complex Sentences

A **complex sentence** consists of one independent clause and one or more dependent clauses. In the following sentences, the dependent clauses are italicized.

When lilacs are in bloom, we love to visit friends in the country. (one dependent clause and one independent clause)

Although it rained last night, we decided to take the path *that led through the woods.* (one independent clause and two dependent clauses)

A relative clause (see page 28) can be the dependent clause in a complex sentence.

I knew the actress *who played that part in the 1980s.*

Punctuation tip: Use a comma after a dependent clause that appears before the main clause.

When the bus arrived, we quickly boarded.

Exercise 4 Writing Complex Sentences

Write six complex sentences. The first five have been started for you.

1. Although he did the work quickly, _____

    _____

2. _____

    because the storm hit.

3. After you go to the party, _____

    _____

4. Because you are smart, _____

    _____

5. _____

    _____ when he turned to leave.

6. _____

    _____

Compound-Complex Sentences

A **compound-complex sentence** consists of two or more independent clauses and one or more dependent clauses.

COMPOUND-COMPLEX SENTENCE	Albert enlisted in the Army, and Robert, who was his older brother, joined him a day later.
INDEPENDENT CLAUSES	Albert enlisted in the Army Robert joined him a day later
DEPENDENT CLAUSE	who was his older brother
COMPOUND-COMPLEX SENTENCE	Because Mr. Roberts was a talented teacher, he was voted Teacher of the Year, and his students prospered.

INDEPENDENT
    CLAUSES   he was voted Teacher of the Year
             his students prospered

DEPENDENT
    CLAUSE   Because Mr. Roberts was a talented teacher

Exercise 5 Writing Compound-Complex Sentences

Write six compound-complex sentences. The first five have been started for you.

1. Because he was my friend, I had to defend him, and I _____

   _____

2. Although he started late, he finished rapidly, and he _____

   _____

3. She had not eaten since the clock struck twelve, and she _____

   _____

4. We didn't realize that he was sick, but _____

   _____

5. If you want to leave, _____

   _____

6. _____

   _____

∿ Chapter Review

Exercise 6 Identifying Types of Sentences

Indicate the kind of sentence by writing the appropriate letter(s) in the blank.

S   simple
CP   compound
CX   complex
CC   compound-complex

_____ 1. The most popular sport in the world is soccer.

_____ 2. People in ancient China and Japan had a form of soccer, and even Rome had a game that resembled soccer.

_____ 3. The game as it is played today got its start in England.

_____ 4. In the Middle Ages, whole towns played soccer on Shrove Tuesday.

_____ 5. Goals were built at opposite ends of town, and hundreds of people who lived in those towns would play on each side.

_____ 6. Such games resembled full-scale brawls.

_____ 7. The first side to score a goal won and was declared village champion.

_____ 8. Then both sides tended to the wounded, and they didn't play again for a whole year.

_____ 9. The rules of the game were written in the late 1800s at British boarding schools.

_____ 10. Now nearly every European country has a national soccer team, and the teams participate in international tournaments.

Exercise 7 Identifying Types of Sentences

Indicate the kind of sentence by writing the appropriate letter(s) in the blank.

S   simple
CP   compound
CX   complex
CC   compound-complex

_____ 1. Leonardo da Vinci was one of the greatest painters of the Italian Renaissance.

_____ 2. His portrait _Mona Lisa_ and his religious scene _The Last Supper_ rank among the most famous pictures ever painted.

_____ 3. Da Vinci was trained to be a painter, but he was also one of the most versatile geniuses in all of history.

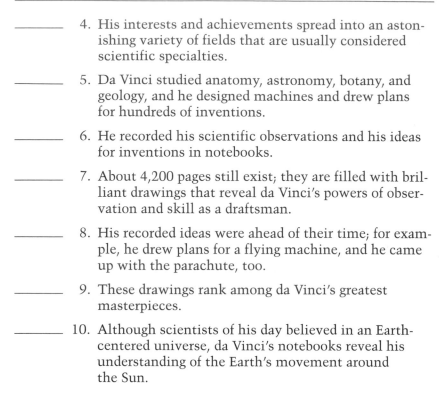

_____ 4. His interests and achievements spread into an astonishing variety of fields that are usually considered scientific specialties.

_____ 5. Da Vinci studied anatomy, astronomy, botany, and geology, and he designed machines and drew plans for hundreds of inventions.

_____ 6. He recorded his scientific observations and his ideas for inventions in notebooks.

_____ 7. About 4,200 pages still exist; they are filled with brilliant drawings that reveal da Vinci's powers of observation and skill as a draftsman.

_____ 8. His recorded ideas were ahead of their time; for example, he drew plans for a flying machine, and he came up with the parachute, too.

_____ 9. These drawings rank among da Vinci's greatest masterpieces.

_____ 10. Although scientists of his day believed in an Earth-centered universe, da Vinci's notebooks reveal his understanding of the Earth's movement around the Sun.

Exercise 8 Identifying Types of Sentences

Indicate the kind of sentence by writing the appropriate letter(s) in the blank.

S   simple
CP   compound
CX   complex
CC   compound-complex

_____ 1. Around 500 BCE, the Mayans began to create their civilization in the southern Gulf Coast region and present-day Guatemala.

_____ 2. The result was remarkable for its brilliant achievements.

_____ 3. Although they had no wheeled vehicles and no beasts of burden such as horses or oxen, they moved great pieces of stone to build their temples.

_____ 4. They had no iron tools; however, because they shaped their stone blocks so skillfully, their pyramids still stand.

_____ 5. The pyramids were the center of Mayan religious ceremonies.

_____ 6. The Mayans built many city-states, and the ruins of at least eighty have been found.

_____ 7. The tallest pyramid was as high as a twenty-story building.

_____ 8. A small temple was constructed at the top, where priests conducted ceremonies.

_____ 9. These pyramids were surrounded by plazas and avenues.

_____ 10. The Mayans were able to build complex structures and to invent an accurate calendar because they knew mathematics well.

4

Combining Sentences, Avoiding Omissions, Achieving Sentence Variety

The simple sentence, the most basic sentence in the English language, can be exceptionally useful and powerful. Some of the greatest statements in literature have been presented in the simple sentence. Its strength is in its singleness of purpose. However, a piece of writing made up of a long series of simple sentences is likely to be monotonous. Moreover, the form may suggest a separateness of ideas that does not serve your purpose well. If your ideas are closely related, some equal in importance and some not, you can combine sentences to show the relationships between your ideas.

If you combine sentences skillfully, you will avoid omissions and achieve a variety of sentence patterns.

∼ Coordination: The Compound Sentence

If you intend to communicate two equally important and closely related ideas, you certainly will want to place them close together, probably in a compound sentence.

Suppose we take two simple sentences that we want to combine:

I am very tired. I worked very hard today.

We have already looked at coordinating conjunctions as a way of joining independent clauses to create compound sentences. Depending on which coordinating conjunction you use, you can show different kinds of relationships. (The following list is arranged according to the FANBOYS acronym. Only the first conjunction joins the original two sentences.)

For shows a reason:
I am very tired, *for* I worked very hard today.

38

And shows equal ideas:
    I am very tired, *and* I want to rest for a few minutes.

Nor indicates a negative choice or alternative:
    I am not tired, *nor* am I hungry right now.

But shows contrast:
    I am very tired, *but* I have no time to rest now.

Or indicates a choice or an alternative:
    I will take a nap, *or* I will go out jogging.

Yet indicates contrast:
    I am very tired, *yet* I am unable to relax.

So points to a result:
    I am very tired, *so* I will take a nap.

Punctuation with Coordinating Conjunctions

When you combine two sentences by using a coordinating conjunction, drop the period, change the capital letter to a small letter, and insert a comma before the coordinating conjunction.

$$\text{Independent clause} \left\{ \begin{array}{l} , for \\ , and \\ , nor \\ , but \\ , or \\ , yet \\ , so \end{array} \right\} \text{independent clause.}$$

Exercise 1 Combining Sentences: Compound

Combine the following pairs of sentences by deleting the first period, changing the capital letter that begins the second sentence to a small letter, and inserting a comma and an appropriate coordinating conjunction from the FANBOYS list. Feel free to reword the sentences as necessary.

1. James Francis "Jim" Thorpe, a Sac and Fox Indian, was born in

   1888 near Prague, Oklahoma. At the age of sixteen, he left

   home to enroll in the Carlisle Indian School in Pennsylvania.

2. He had had little experience playing football. He led his small

   college to victories against championship teams.

3. He had scarcely heard of other sports. He golfed in the 70s,

   bowled above 200, and played varsity basketball and lacrosse.

4. In the 1912 Olympic Games for amateur athletes at

   Stockholm, Jim Thorpe entered the two most rigorous events,

   the decathlon and the pentathlon. He won both.

5. King Gustav V of Sweden told him, "You, Sir, are the greatest

   athlete in the world." Jim Thorpe said, "Thanks, King."

6. Later it was said he had once been paid fifteen dollars a week to

   play baseball, making him a professional athlete. The Olympic

   medals were taken from him.

7. Soon a Major League baseball scout did offer Thorpe a

   respectable contract. He played in the National League for

   six seasons.

8. Not content to play only one sport, he also earned a good salary

   for that time in professional football. After competing for

   fifteen years, he said he had never played for the money.

9. Many regard Jim Thorpe as the greatest athlete of the

   twentieth century. He excelled in many sports at the highest

   levels of athletic competition.

10. Off the playing fields, he was known by his friends as a modest, quiet man. On the fields, he was a person of joyful combat.

Semicolons and Conjunctive Adverbs

We have also already looked at using a semicolon to join independent clauses to make a compound sentence. Here are two more simple sentences to combine:

> We were late. We missed the first act.

We can make one compound sentence using these simple sentences by joining the two clauses with a semicolon:

> We were late; we missed the first act.

We can also use words called conjunctive adverbs after semicolons to make the relationship between the two clauses clearer. Look at how the conjunctive adverb *therefore* adds the idea of "as a result."

> We were late; *therefore*, we missed the first act.

Conjunctive adverbs include the following words and phrases: *also, consequently, furthermore, hence, however, in fact, moreover, nevertheless, now, on the other hand, otherwise, soon, therefore, similarly, then, thus.*

When you coordinate ideas with conjunctive adverbs, consider the meanings of these words:

> As a result of: *therefore, consequently, hence, thus, then*
> To the contrary or with reservation: *however, nevertheless, otherwise, on the other hand*
> In addition to: *moreover, also*
> To emphasize or specify: *in fact, for example*
> To compare: *similarly*

Punctuation with Semicolons and Conjunctive Adverbs

When you combine two sentences by using a semicolon, replace the period with a semicolon and change the capital letter that begins the second sentence to a small letter. If you wish to use a conjunctive adverb, insert it after the semicolon and usually put a comma after it. (However, usually no comma follows *then, now, thus,* and *soon.*)

The first letters of ten common conjunctive adverbs make up the acronym HOTSHOT CAT.

Independent clause $\left\{ \begin{array}{l} \textit{; however,} \\ \textit{; otherwise,} \\ \textit{; therefore,} \\ \textit{; similarly,} \\ \textit{; hence} \\ \textit{; on the other hand,} \\ \textit{; then} \\ \textit{; consequently,} \\ \textit{; also,} \\ \textit{; thus} \end{array} \right\}$ independent clause.

Exercise 2 Combining Sentences: Compound

Combine the following pairs of sentences by replacing the first period with a semicolon, changing the capital letter that begins the second sentence to a small letter, and inserting a conjunctive adverb if appropriate. Consider the list of conjunctive adverbs (HOTSHOT CAT and others). Do not use a conjunctive adverb in every sentence.

1. The legendary island of Atlantis has fascinated people for centuries. It probably never existed.

2. According to the Greek writer Plato, the people of Atlantis were very ambitious and warlike. They planned to conquer all of the Mediterranean.

3. Initially, they were successful in subduing areas to the west. They became wealthy.

4. Then the people of Atlantis became proud. They became corrupt and wicked.

5. They were confident and attacked Athens. Athens and its allies defeated the invaders.

6. The story of Atlantis is probably just a tale. Many people have believed it.

7. Some writers have tried to link the legend with such real places as America and the Canary Islands. No link has been found.

8. The Minoan civilization on Crete was destroyed by tidal waves. A similar fate may have befallen Atlantis.

9. Some people speculate about a volcanic explosion on Atlantis. A volcanic eruption did destroy part of the island Thera in the Eastern Mediterranean in 1500 BCE.

10. Some writers have conjectured that American Indians migrated to the New World by way of Atlantis. Archaeologists dispute that idea.

∿ Subordination: The Complex Sentence

Whereas a compound sentence contains independent clauses that are equally important and closely related, a complex sentence combines ideas of unequal value. The following two sentences can be combined as either a compound sentence or a complex sentence, depending on whether the writer thinks the ideas are of equal value.

My neighbors are considerate. They never play loud music.

Combined as a compound sentence, suggesting that the ideas are of equal value, the new sentence looks like this:

My neighbors are considerate, and they never play loud music.

<table>
<tr><td>independent clause
(main idea)</td><td>independent clause
(main idea)</td></tr>
</table>

Here are the same two ideas combined as a complex sentence, suggesting that the ideas are of unequal value:

<u>Because my neighbors are considerate</u>, <u>they never play loud music.</u>
    dependent clause   independent clause
   (less important idea)   (main idea)

Although both the compound and complex forms are correct, the complex form conveys the ideas more precisely in this sentence because one idea does seem to be more important—one idea depends on the other.

Thus if you have two sentences with closely related ideas and one is clearly more important than the other, consider combining them in a complex sentence. Compare these two paragraphs:

- Version 1 contains six simple sentences, implying that the ideas are of equal value:

  (1) I was very upset. (2) The Fourth of July fireworks were especially loud. (3) My dog ran away. (4) The animal control officer made his morning rounds. (5) He found my dog in another part of town. (6) I was relieved.

- Version 2 consists of two simple sentences and two complex sentences, showing that some ideas are more important than others:

  (1) I was very upset. (2) Because the Fourth of July fireworks were especially loud, my dog ran away. (3) When the animal control officer made his morning rounds, he found my dog in another part of town. (4) I was relieved.

You will probably consider Version 2 superior to Version 1. Sentences 2 and 3 are closely related, but 3 is more important. And sentences 4 and 5 are closely related, but 5 is more important. The revision made each pair into a complex sentence.

Although you could combine sentences 1 and 2, the result would be illogical because the wrong idea would be conveyed:

  I was very upset because the Fourth of July fireworks were especially loud.

The person was very upset because the dog ran away, not because the fireworks were especially loud.

As you learned in Chapter 3, a complex sentence is composed of one independent clause and one or more dependent clauses. In combining two independent clauses to write a complex sentence, your first step is to decide on a word that will best show the relationship between the clauses. Words that show the relationship of a dependent clause to an independent one are called subordinating conjunctions. The italicized words in the sentences that follow are subordinating conjunctions. Consider the meaning as well as the placement of each one.

> *Because* the storm hit, the game was canceled.
>
> *After* the storm passed, the clown dogs began to bark.
>
> *When* she read her poem, they were moved to fits of hysterics.
>
> He did not volunteer to work on the holiday, *although* the pay was good.
>
> No one has visited her *since* she moved into town.
>
> They decided to wait *until* the cows came home.
>
> They refused to work *unless* they were allowed to wear chef's hats.
>
> *Before* the session ended, all the "hep cats" blew some sweet sounds.

Other subordinating conjunctions include the following:

as	if	so that	whereas
as if	in order that	than	wherever
even if	provided that	whenever	whether
even though	rather than	where	while

Punctuation with Subordinating Conjunctions

If the dependent clause comes *before* the main clause, set it off with a comma.

> Before you dive, be sure there is water in the pool.

If the dependent clause comes *after* or *within* the main clause, set it off only if the clause is not necessary to the meaning of the main clause or if the dependent clause begins with the word *although* or *though*.

> Be sure there is water in the pool *before* you dive.
>
> We went home *after* the concert had ended.
>
> Yogi continued to brush, *although* he had painted the cabinet twice.

You have already learned that a relative clause—one that starts with a relative pronoun like *that*, *which*, or *who*—can be the dependent clause in a sentence. If we look at the two sentences we started with, we can see how they can be combined using a relative clause.

My neighbors are considerate. They never play loud music.

Combined as a complex sentence with a relative clause as the dependent clause, the new sentence looks like this:

My neighbors, who are considerate, never play loud music.
dependent clause

Punctuation with Relative Pronouns

Set the dependent clause off with commas when it is not necessary to the sentence. Do not set the clause off if it is necessary for the meaning of the sentence.

Everyone *who tries* will pass this class. (The dependent clause is necessary because one would not say, "Everyone will pass this class.")

Kumar, *who tries*, will pass this class. (The dependent clause is not necessary because one can say, "Kumar will pass this class.")

The relative pronoun *which* usually refers to things. The word *which* almost always indicates that a clause is not necessary for the meaning of the sentence. Therefore, a clause beginning with *which* is almost always set off by commas.

My car, *which is ten years old*, has a flat tire.

The relative pronoun *that* also usually refers to things. However, the word *that* almost always indicates that the clause *is* necessary for the meaning of the sentence. Therefore, a clause beginning with *that* is *not* set off by commas.

The car *that* has a flat tire is ten years old.

The relative pronouns *who* and *whom*, as well as *whoever* and *whomever*, usually refer to people. Clauses that begin with those relative pronouns are not set off by commas if they are necessary for the meaning of the sentence; if they are not necessary, they are set off.

A person *who* has a way with words is often quoted. (necessary for the meaning of the sentence)

My uncle, *whom* I quote often, has a way with words. (not necessary for the meaning of the sentence)

Exercise 3 Combining Sentences: Complex

Combine the following pairs of sentences into one complex sentence. Insert an appropriate subordinating conjunction or relative pronoun, add or fix punctuation, and make other minor changes as needed. Sentences that should be combined by using a relative pronoun are indicated.

1. (relative pronoun) The freeway congestion was under study. The problem occurred every Friday at noon.

2. The vacationers had a good time. The bears destroyed a few tents and ate people's food.

3. The teenagers loved their senior prom. The band played badly.

4. Farmers gathered for miles around. Jeff had grown a fifty-pound cucumber.

5. Backseat drivers make unwanted suggestions in the nag-proof model. They can be ejected from the vehicle.

6. (relative pronoun) The marriage counselor gave bad advice. He charged only half price.

7. (relative pronoun) The robots would not do their work. They needed fresh batteries.

8. The hurricane was expected to hit during the night. The residents checked their flashlights.

9. The ice sculptor displayed his work in the dining hall. The

customers applauded.

10. Someone stole the artwork of ice. No evidence was found.

∿ Coordination and Subordination: The Compound-Complex Sentence

At times you may want to show the relationship of three or more ideas within one sentence. If that relationship involves two or more main ideas and one or more supporting ideas, the combination can be stated in a compound-complex sentence (two or more independent clauses and one or more dependent clauses).

<u>Before Carson learned how to operate a computer,</u>
dependent clause

<u>he had trouble with his typewritten assignments,</u>
independent clause

but now <u>he produces clean, attractive material.</u>
independent clause

In our previous discussion of the complex sentence, we presented this group of six sentences:

I was very upset. The Fourth of July fireworks were especially loud. My dog ran away. The animal control officer made his morning rounds. He found my dog in another part of town. I was relieved.

We then converted the group of six sentences to four:

I was very upset. Because the Fourth of July fireworks were especially loud, my dog ran away. When the animal control officer made his morning rounds, he found my dog in another part of town. I was relieved.

If we wanted to show an even closer relationship of ideas we could combine the two complex sentences in this way (the italicized sentence is compound-complex):

I was very upset. *Because the Fourth of July fireworks were especially loud, my dog ran away; but when the animal control officer made his morning rounds, he found my dog in another part of town.* I was relieved.

Punctuation of Complicated Compound or Compound-Complex Sentences

If a compound or compound-complex sentence has one or more commas in the first clause, you may want to use a semicolon before the coordinating conjunction between the two clauses. Its purpose is to show the reader very clearly the division between the two independent clauses. The preceding example illustrates this use of the semicolon.

Exercise 4 Combining Sentences: Compound-Complex

Combine each group of sentences into one compound-complex sentence. Use the rules of sentence combining and punctuation discussed in this chapter.

1. Helen Keller suffered a serious childhood illness. She became blind and deaf. At first her parents did not know what to do.

2. Her parents would not give up despite discouraging advice. They advertised for a teacher. A tutor named Anne Sullivan agreed to help.

3. Young Helen began to discover the world through her sense of touch. She learned the alphabet. She started connecting words with objects.

4. Her physical condition was irreversible. Her progress was rapid. In three years she could read Braille.

5. She could not talk. She used sign language for speech. She used a special typewriter to write.

6. She reached the age of ten. She took speech lessons from a teacher of the deaf. In six years she could speak well enough to be understood.

7. She attended college. She still needed help. Anne Sullivan continued as her tutor and interpreter.

8. She graduated from college with honors. She became involved in programs to help the deaf and blind communicate. She wrote books and articles about problems of the disabled.

9. The effects of World War II presented special problems. Helen Keller helped disabled people in other countries. She helped soldiers blinded in the war.

10. Helen Keller died in 1968. She had an international reputation as a humanitarian. Her books had been translated into more than fifty languages.

∼ Other Ways to Combine Ideas

In this chapter you have learned how to combine simple sentences into compound, complex, and compound-complex sentences that show the coordination and subordination of ideas. There are other methods of combining ideas. Here are four you may want to use in your own writing:

1. Use an **appositive**, which is a noun or a noun phrase that immediately follows a noun or pronoun and renames it.

> Susan is the leading scorer on the team. Susan is a quick and strong player.
>
> Susan, *a quick and strong player*, is the leading scorer on the team.

2. Use a **prepositional phrase**, a preposition followed by a noun or pronoun object.

> Dolly Parton wrote a song about a coat. The coat had many colors.
>
> Dolly Parton wrote a song about a coat *of many colors.*

3. Drop the subject in the sentence that follows, and combine the sentences.

> Some items are too damaged for recycling. They must be disposed of.
>
> Some items are too damaged for recycling *and* must be disposed of.

4. Use a **participial phrase**, a group of words that includes a participle, which is a verbal that usually ends in *-ing* or *-ed*.

> Miguel rowed smoothly. He reached the shore.
>
> *Rowing smoothly*, Miguel reached the shore.

∼ Omissions: When Parts Are Missing

The omission of a word or words may occur during sentence combining. Do not omit words that are needed to make your sentences clear and logical. Of the many types of undesirable construction in which necessary words are omitted, the following are the most common:

1. **Subjects.** Do not omit a necessary subject in a sentence with two verbs.

> ILLOGICAL The cost of the car was $12,000 but would easily last me through college. (subject of *last*)
>
> LOGICAL The cost of the car was $12,000, but the car would easily last me through college.

2. **Verbs.** Do not omit verbs that are needed because of a change in the number of the subject or a change of tense.

> ILLOGICAL The bushes were trimmed and the grass mowed. (verb of *grass*)
>
> LOGICAL The bushes were trimmed and the grass was mowed.

> ILLOGICAL   True honesty always has and always will be admired by most people. (tense)
>
> LOGICAL   True honesty always has been and always will be admired by most people.

3. ***That* as a conjunction.** The conjunction *that* should not be omitted from a dependent clause if there is danger of misreading the sentence.

> MISLEADING   We believed Marcos, if not stopped, would hurt himself. (*that* after *believed*)
>
> CLEAR   We believed that Marcos, if not stopped, would hurt himself.

4. **Prepositions.** Do not omit prepositions in idiomatic phrases, in expressions of time, and in parallel phrases.

> ILLOGICAL   Weekends the campus is deserted. (time)
>
> LOGICAL   During weekends the campus is deserted.
>
> ILLOGICAL   I have neither love nor patience with untrained dogs. (parallel phrases)
>
> LOGICAL   I have neither love for nor patience with untrained dogs.
>
> ILLOGICAL   Macarena's illness was something we heard only after her recovery. (*about* after *heard*)
>
> LOGICAL   Macarena's illness was something we heard about only after her recovery.

Exercise 5   Correcting Omissions

Identify the kinds of omissions by writing one of the following words in the blank to the left: subject, verb, conjunction, preposition. Insert the necessary words in the sentences.

_____   1. Jessica had neither love nor patience with small pets.

_____   2. Because Rudy was careless, a branch caught on the trigger of his gun, and went off.

_____   3. In the newspaper, the radio, and TV, the story was the same.

_____ 4. We saw the car, if not stopped, would hit the tree.

_____ 5. Because Lana had not worked that summer, money was scarce in the fall and expenses burdensome.

_____ 6. Richard's ignorance was one of the things that we learned on the trip.

_____ 7. We believed the lie, if not revealed, would harm people.

_____ 8. The truck was creeping up the hill, and had no thought at all of the traffic behind.

_____ 9. I do not believe and never have that a person's life is not his or her own responsibility.

_____ 10. When Leonardo got his second wind, his breathing slowed, and was able to go on running without fatigue.

⌒ Variety in Sentences: Types, Order, Length, Beginnings

Sentences can be written in a variety of ways to achieve freshness and clarity. Much of this polishing takes place during revision, and often during sentence combining. Here are a few techniques for the main variations.

Types

You have learned that all four types of sentences are sound. Your task as a writer is to decide which one to use for a particular thought. That decision may not be made until you revise your composition. Then you can choose on the basis of the relationship of ideas:

Simple: a single idea
Compound: two closely related ideas
Complex: one idea more important than the other
Compound-complex: a combination of the two parts

These types were all covered in Chapter 3. This chapter provides further practice, as you combine sentences.

Order

You will choose the order of parts and information according to what you want to emphasize. Typically the most emphatic location is at the end of any unit.

Length

Uncluttered and direct, short sentences commonly draw attention. Because that focus occurs only when they stand out from longer sentences, however, you would usually avoid a series of short sentences.

Beginnings

A long series of sentences with each beginning containing a subject followed by a verb may become monotonous. Consider beginning sentences in different ways:

> **With a prepositional phrase:** *In the distance* a dog barked.
> **With a transitional connective (conjunctive adverb) such as *then, however,* or *therefore*:** *Then* the game was over.
> **With a coordinating conjunction such as *and* or *but*:** *But* no one moved for three minutes.
> **With a dependent clause:** *Although Reggie wanted a new Corvette,* he settled for a used Ford Taurus.
> **With an adverb:** *Carefully* Sabrina removed the thorn from the lion's paw.

Exercise 6   Providing Sentence Variety

Revise the following passage to achieve better sentence variety through changes in types of sentences, order of information, length of sentences, and beginnings of sentences. Also, take care to avoid omission, and combine sentences for improved expression. Compare your revisions with those of others in your class. There is no single correct way of making these changes.

Power Rangers to the Rescue

Leewan Yeomans

I do promotions on the weekends for TV's "Power Rangers." I'm Trini. She's supposed to be Chinese. I'm Chinese American, the kids think I'm the real Ranger when I remove my mask. I've never

felt very much like a Ranger except for one occasion. It was a
weekend promotion, held at a park. We were doing our routine.
I looked around and saw a little boy collapse. He had probably
been in distress for a while. Wearing the mask, I could hardly see
anything. Anyway, this little boy was lying there, thrashing
around and trying to throw up. No one was doing anything.
The Pink Ranger started running around trying to find the child's
parents. I ran over when no one came to the aid of the boy, took
off my mask, and put my finger in his mouth to clear his throat.
There I found the problem. He had been chewing on, or maybe
blowing, a long balloon. He had swallowed it. I pulled it out of his
throat. It was almost a foot long. The whole spectacle must have
looked like a magic trick. The child still wasn't breathing well.
The paramedics were called. They quickly helped him back to
good health. His parents, who lived across the street, came
to carry him home. We Rangers put our masks back on. The
audience cheered us as if we had planned the whole scene.
We resumed our routine. It was just another day of work for
the Power Rangers.

◠ Chapter Review

Exercise 7 Combining Sentences

*Combine each pair of sentences into a single sentence by using any
pattern.*

1. Cobras are among the most feared of all snakes. They are not

   the deadliest of all snakes.

2. Cobras do not coil before they strike. They cannot strike over a long distance.

3. Cobras do not have a hood. They flatten their neck by moving their ribs when they are nervous or frightened.

4. Cobras inject venom with their fangs. They spit venom at their victims.

5. Human beings will not die from the venom that has been spit. It can cause blindness if it is not washed from the eyes.

6. A person can die from a cobra bite. Death may come in only a few hours.

7. Snake charmers have long worked with cobras. They use a snake, a basket, and a flute.

8. The snakes cannot *hear* the music. They respond to the rhythmic movements of the charmers.

9. The snake charmers are hardly ever in danger of being bitten. They defang the cobras or sew their mouths shut.

10. Most cobras will flee from people. They attack if they are cornered or if they are guarding their eggs.

Exercise 8 Combining Sentences

Combine each pair or group of sentences into a single sentence by using any pattern.

1. The Mercury Comet was judged the winner. It had imitation zebra-skin seat covers. It had an eight-ball shift knob.

2. Koko had a great plan to make some money. She had financial problems. She could not implement her plan.

3. The mixture could not be discussed openly. Competitors were curious. Corporate spies were everywhere.

4. Babette's bowling ball is special. It is red and green. It is decorated with her email address in metal-flake.

5. The young bagpiper liked Scottish food. He enjoyed doing Scottish dances. Wearing a kilt in winter left him cold.

6. Ruby missed the alligator farm. She fondly remembered the hissing and snapping of the beasts as they scrambled for raw meat. Her neighbors were indifferent to the loss.

7. Many people are pleased to purchase items with food preservatives. Others are fearful. They think these chemicals may also preserve consumers.

8. Lauren loves her new in-line roller skates. They look and perform much like ice skates. They are not as safe as her conventional roller skates.

9. Fish sold at Discount Fish Market were not of the highest

    quality. Some of them had been dead for days without

    refrigeration. They were suitable only for bait.

10. Earl wanted to impress his date. He splashed on some cologne.

    He put on his motorcycle leathers and a flying scarf.

Exercise 9   Combining Sentences

Use appropriate methods to combine sentences as needed. Add and delete words sparingly.

Muhammad Ali was arguably the greatest heavyweight

boxing champion. He won the title on four occasions. He loved to

perform for the press. He made up sayings and poems about

himself and his opponents. He once said he would "float like a

butterfly and sting like a bee." Ali announced that he would win

each fight. He even named the round. He became a Black Muslim.

He refused induction into the armed services. He was convicted of

a crime for having done so. As a result he lost his championship.

Later the decision was reversed by the U.S. Supreme Court. He

won back the championship by defeating George Foreman in 1974.

In 1978 he lost it to Leon Spinks. He regained it the next year. He

retired in 1980. He soon returned to the ring once more to fight for

the championship. He quit for good.

5

Correcting Fragments, Comma Splices, and Run-Ons

In Chapters 1 and 2, you learned about parts of speech and subjects and verbs. In Chapters 3 and 4, you identified and wrote different kinds of sentences. With the information you now have, you will be able to spot and correct three problems that sometimes creep into what is otherwise good writing. Those problems are sentence fragments, comma splices, and run-on sentences.

Fragments

A correct sentence signals completeness. The structure and punctuation provide those signals. For example, if I say to you, "She left in a hurry," you do not necessarily expect me to say anything else, but if I say, "In a hurry," you do. If I say, "Tomorrow I will give you a quiz on the reading assignment," and I leave the room, you will merely take note of my words. But if I say, "Tomorrow when I give you a quiz on the reading assignment," and leave the room, you will probably be annoyed, and you may even chase after me and ask me to finish my sentence. Those examples illustrate the difference between completeness and incompleteness.

A **fragment** is a word or group of words without a subject ("Is going to town."), without a verb ("He going to town."), or without both ("Going to town."). A fragment can also be a group of words with a subject and verb that cannot stand alone ("When he goes to town."). Although the punctuation signals a sentence (a capital letter at the beginning and a period at the end), the structure of a fragment signals incompleteness. If you were to say or write a fragment to someone, that person would expect you to go on and finish the idea.

59

Other specific examples of common unacceptable fragments are the following:

- *Dependent clause only*: When she came.
- *Phrase(s) only*: Waiting there for some help.
- *No subject in main clause*: Went to the library.
- *No verb in main clause*: She being the only person there.

Dependent Clauses as Fragments: Clauses with Subordinating Conjunctions

In Chapter 3, you learned that words such as *because, after, although, since,* and *before* (see page 28 for a more complete list) are subordinating conjunctions, words that show the relationship of a dependent clause to an independent one. A dependent clause punctuated like a sentence (capital letter at the beginning; period at the end) is a sentence fragment.

While the ship was sinking.

You can choose one of many ways to fix that kind of fragment.

INCORRECT   They continued to dance. *While the ship was sinking.*

CORRECT   They continued to dance *while the ship was sinking.*

CORRECT   *While the ship was sinking,* they continued to dance.

CORRECT   The ship was sinking. They continued to dance.

CORRECT   The ship was sinking; they continued to dance.

In the first two correct sentences above, the dependent clause *while the ship was sinking* has been attached to an independent clause. In the next two sentences, the subordinating conjunction *while* has been omitted. The two independent clauses can then stand alone as sentences or as parts of a sentence, joined by a semicolon.

Dependent Clauses as Fragments: Clauses with Relative Pronouns

You also learned in Chapter 3 that words such as *that, which,* and *who* can function as relative pronouns, words that relate a clause back to a noun or pronoun in the sentence. Relative clauses are dependent. If they are punctuated as sentences (begin with a capital letter; end with a period), they are incorrect. They are really sentence fragments.

Which is lying on the floor.

The best way to fix such a fragment is to attach it as close as possible to the noun to which it refers.

> INCORRECT   That new red sweater is mine. *Which is lying on the floor.*
>
> CORRECT   The new red sweater, *which is lying on the floor,* is mine.

Reminder: Some relative clauses are restrictive (necessary to the meaning of the sentence) and should not be set off with commas. Some are nonrestrictive (not necessary to the meaning of the sentence), as in the example above, and are set off by commas.

Phrases as Fragments

Although a phrase may carry an idea, a phrase is a fragment because it is incomplete in structure. It lacks both a subject and a verb. In Chapter 2 we looked at verbal phrases and prepositional phrases, and in Chapter 4 we briefly discussed appositive phrases.

Verbal Phrase

> INCORRECT   *Having studied hard all evening.* John decided to retire.
>
> CORRECT   *Having studied hard all evening,* John decided to retire.

The italicized part of this example is a verbal phrase. As you learned in Chapter 2, a verbal is verblike without being a verb in sentence structure. Verbals include verb parts of speech ending in -ed and -ing. To correct a verbal phrase fragment, attach it to a complete sentence (an independent clause). When the phrase begins the sentence, it is usually set off by a comma.

Prepositional Phrase

> INCORRECT   *After the last snow* The workers built the road.
>
> CORRECT   *After the last snow,* the workers built the road.

In this example, the fragment is a prepositional phrase—a group of words beginning with a preposition, such as *in, on, of, at,* and *with,* that connects a noun or pronoun object to the rest of the sentence. To correct a prepositional phrase fragment, attach it to a complete sentence (an independent clause). If the prepositional phrase is long and begins the sentence, it is usually set off by a comma.

Appositive Phrase

INCORRECT   Kevin lived in the small town of Whitman. *A busy industrial center near Boston.* (nonessential)

CORRECT   Kevin lived in the small town of Whitman, *a busy industrial center near Boston.*

INCORRECT   Many readers admire the work of the nineteenth-century American poet. *Emily Dickinson.* (essential)

CORRECT   Many readers admire the work of the nineteenth-century American poet *Emily Dickinson.*

In these examples, the fragment is an appositive phrase—a group of words following a noun or pronoun and renaming it. To correct an appositive phrase fragment, connect it to a complete sentence (an independent clause). An appositive phrase fragment is set off by a comma or by commas only if it is not essential to the sentence.

Fragments as Word Groups Without Subjects or Without Verbs

INCORRECT   Jermain studied many long hours. *And received the highest grade in the class.* (without subject)

CORRECT   Jermain studied many long hours *and received the highest grade in the class.*

INCORRECT   *Few children living in that section of the country.* (without verb)

CORRECT   *Few children live in that section of the country.*

Each conventional sentence must have an independent clause, meaning a word or a group of words that contains a subject and a verb and that can stand alone. As you may recall from the discussion of subjects in Chapter 2, a command or direction sentence, such as "Think," has an understood subject of *you.*

Acceptable Fragments

Sometimes fragments are used intentionally. When we speak, we often use the following fragments:

- *Interjections*: Great! Hooray! Whoa! Right!
- *Exclamations*: What a day! How terrible! What a bother! Are you serious!

- *Greetings*: Hello. Good morning. Good night. Good evening.
- *Questions*: What for? Why not? Where to?
- *Informal conversation*: (What time is it?) Eight o'clock. Really.

In novels, plays, and short stories, fragments are often used in conversation among characters. However, unless you are writing fiction, you need to be able to identify fragments in your college assignments and turn those fragments into complete sentences.

Exercise 1 Identifying Fragments

Identify each of the following as a fragment (FRAG) or a complete sentence (OK).

_____ 1. Asia, which developed much earlier than the West.

_____ 2. More than five thousand years ago, Asia had an advanced civilization.

_____ 3. People there who invented writing and created literature.

_____ 4. Involved in the development of science, agriculture, and religion.

_____ 5. The birthplace of the major religions of the world.

_____ 6. The most common religion in Asia being Hinduism.

_____ 7. The second most common religion is Islam.

_____ 8. Asia is the most populous continent.

_____ 9. With almost four billion people.

_____ 10. Hong Kong and Bangladesh, which are among the most densely populated places in the world.

Exercise 2 Correcting Fragments

Underline and correct each fragment. Some items may be correct as is.

1. When Leroy Robert Paige was seven years old. He was carrying luggage at a railroad station in Mobile, Alabama.

2. He was a clever young fellow. Who invented a contraption for carrying four satchels (small suitcases) at one time.

3. After he did that. He became known as Satchel Paige.

4. His fame rests on his being arguably the best baseball pitcher. Who ever played the game.

5. Because of the so-called Jim Crow laws. He, as an African American, was not allowed to play in the Major Leagues. Until 1948 after the Major League color barrier was broken.

6. By that time he was already forty-two. Although he was in excellent condition.

7. He had pitched. Wherever he could, mainly touring around the country.

8. When he faced Major Leaguers in exhibition games. He almost always won.

9. Because people liked to see him pitch. He pitched almost every day. While he was on tour.

10. One year he won 104 games. During his career he pitched 55 no-hitters and won more than 2,000 games.

11. He pitched his last game in the majors at the age of fifty-nine.

12. In 1971, he was the first African American player. Who was voted into the Baseball Hall of Fame in a special category for those. Who played in the old Negro Leagues.

Exercise 3 Correcting Fragments

Underline and correct each fragment.

1. Although Woody Guthrie had a hard life. His songs are filled with hope.

2. His autobiography, *Bound for Glory,* tells of this free-spirited man. Who saw boomtown oil fields dry up and crops wither in the dust bowl.

3. Many people knew him only as the author of "This Land Is Your Land." Which is often treated as a second national anthem.

4. Because he was honest and would say what he thought. He was often out of work.

5. Cisco Houston said, "Woody is a man. Who writes two or three ballads before breakfast every morning."

6. The hobo, the migrant worker, the merchant marine, the sign painter, the labor agitator, the musician in New York City with his hat on the sidewalk—Woody was a restless traveler. Whose life was as varied as his song bag.

7. Some of his best songs are about his experience during the days of the Great Depression. When he was an unofficial spokesperson for migrant workers in the West.

8. Arlo Guthrie, Woody's son, achieved his own fame. While he carried on the folk music tradition of his father.

9. Woody's song "Pretty Boy Floyd" was recorded by Bob Dylan. Who modeled his early style on that of Woody and once referred to himself as a "Woody Guthrie jukebox."

10. A simple farmer once said to a reporter, "I'll always remember Woody as the man. Who said, 'Some men will rob you with a six-gun and some with a fountain pen.'"

Exercise 4 Correcting Fragments

Correct the fragments in any way you wish. Many can be fixed by combining word groups in this list. Write your complete sentences in the space provided.

1. Asia having many ethnic groups.

2. Including the Chinese, the Indians, the Arabs, the Turks, and the Jews.

3. The Chinese have different groups.

4. Speaking many dialects.

5. Although they have different dialects.

6. There is a national language.

7. A language called Mandarin.

8. Cultural differences exist in Taiwan.

9. The main difference being between the Chinese from the mainland and the Taiwanese.

10. Despite the differences, all Chinese have much culture in common.

~~/ Comma Splices and Run-Ons

The comma splice and the run-on are two other kinds of faulty "sentences" that give false signals to the reader. In each instance the punctuation suggests that there is only one sentence, but, in fact, there is material for two.

The **comma splice** consists of two independent clauses with only a comma between them:

> *The weather was disappointing,* we canceled the picnic. (A comma by itself cannot join two independent clauses.)

The **run-on** differs from the comma splice in only one respect: it has no comma between the independent clauses. Therefore, the run-on is two independent clauses with *nothing* between them:

> *The weather was disappointing* we canceled the picnic. (Independent clauses must be properly connected.)

Because an independent clause can stand by itself as a sentence and because two independent clauses must be properly linked, you can use a simple technique to identify the comma splice and the run-on. If you see a sentence that you think may contain one of these two errors, ask yourself this question: "Can I insert a period at some place in the word group and still have a sentence on either side?" If the answer is yes and there is no word such as *and* or *but* following the inserted period, then you have a comma splice or a run-on to correct. In our previous examples of the comma splice and the run-on, we could insert a period after the word *disappointing* in each case, and we would still have an independent clause— therefore, a sentence—on either side.

Correcting Comma Splices and Run-Ons

Once you identify a comma splice or a run-on in your writing, you need to correct it. Use one of these four different ways to fix these common sentence problems: use a comma and a coordinating conjunction, use a subordinating conjunction, use a semicolon, or make each clause a separate sentence.

Use a Comma and a Coordinating Conjunction

INCORRECT   We canceled the picnic the weather was disappointing. (run-on)

CORRECT   We canceled the picnic, *for* the weather was disappointing. (Here we inserted a comma and the coordinating conjunction *for.*)

Knowing the seven coordinating conjunctions will help you in writing sentences and correcting sentence problems. Remember the acronym FANBOYS: *for, and, nor, but, or, yet, so.*

Exercise 5 Correcting Comma Splices and Run-Ons

Identify each word group as a comma splice (CS), a run-on (RO), or a complete sentence (OK), and correct the errors using commas and coordinating conjunctions.

                                    and
EXAMPLE: _CS_ He did the assignment, ^his boss gave him a bonus.

_____   1. In 1846, a group of eighty-two settlers headed for California with much optimism, a hard road lay ahead.

_____   2. They had expected to cross the mountains before winter they were in good spirits.

_____ 3. They would not arrive in California before winter, nor would some of them get there at all.

_____ 4. When they encountered a heavy snowstorm, they stopped to spend the winter they still thought they would be safe.

_____ 5. They made crude shelters of logs and branches some also used moss and earth.

_____ 6. They had trouble managing, they had not encountered such problems before.

_____ 7. They ran out of regular food they ate roots, mice, shoe leather, and their horses.

_____ 8. Thirty-five members of the Donner Party died that winter the survivors were so hungry that they ate the dead bodies.

_____ 9. They were weak, sick, and depressed they did not give up.

_____ 10. Fifteen people set out to get help seven survived and returned to rescue friends and relatives.

Exercise 6 Correcting Comma Splices and Run-Ons

Identify each word group as a comma splice (CS), a run-on (RO), or a complete sentence (OK), and correct the errors using commas and coordinating conjunctions.

_____ 1. Comedian Woody Allen once observed that no one gets out of this world alive, we all know that no human is immortal.

_____ 2. But several famous dead people have managed to continue to *look* alive they (or their admirers) had their bodies preserved and put on display.

_____ 3. Philosopher Jeremy Bentham wanted his body preserved, his wishes were carried out when he died in 1832.

_____   4. Bentham left a lot of money to London's University College, the college couldn't have the money unless it agreed to let Bentham's body attend its annual board of directors meetings.

_____   5. Bentham's dressed-up body was posed sitting in an armchair in his hand was his favorite walking stick.

_____   6. Every year for ninety-two years, the college complied with Bentham's instructions the board's minutes for those years record Bentham as "present but not voting."

_____   7. Bentham's body is still at University College, it's on display now in a permanent exhibit.

_____   8. V. I. Lenin, leader of the former Soviet Union, has been dead and on display since 1924 Russians and tourists can still visit his lifelike body enclosed in a glass coffin in Moscow.

_____   9. The corpse of People's Republic of China founder Mao Zedong was preserved for posterity, too, in his mausoleum, an elevator raises his glass coffin from underground to a public viewing area every morning.

_____   10. Other famous people turned into modern mummies were national leaders Joseph Stalin, Eva Perón, and Ho Chi Minh, and opera singer Enrico Caruso.

Use a Subordinating Conjunction

INCORRECT   The weather was disappointing, we canceled the picnic.

CORRECT   *Because* the weather was disappointing, we canceled the picnic.

By inserting the subordinating conjunction *because,* you can transform the first independent clause into a dependent clause and correct the comma splice. Knowing common subordinating conjunctions will help you in writing sentences and correcting sentence problems. Here is a list of the subordinating conjunctions you saw in Chapters 3 and 4. Each of these words indicates a particular relationship between the ideas being connected.

after	if	until
although	in order that	when
as	provided that	whenever
as if	rather than	where
because	since	whereas
before	so that	wherever
even if	than	whether
even though	unless	while

Exercise 7 Correcting Comma Splices and Run-Ons

Identify each word group as a comma splice (CS), a run-on (RO), or a complete sentence (OK), and correct the errors by making a dependent clause.

_____ 1. Jesse Owens won four gold medals in the 1936 Olympics he became a famous person.

_____ 2. The 1936 Olympics were held in Nazi Germany Owens was placed at a disadvantage.

_____ 3. Hitler believed in the superiority of the Aryans, he thought Owens would lose.

_____ 4. Jesse Owens won Hitler showed his disappointment openly.

_____ 5. Owens broke a record for the 200-meter race that had stood for thirty-six years.

_____ 6. Owens then jumped a foot farther than others in the long jump Hitler left the stadium.

_____ 7. Before the day was at last over, Owens had also won gold medals in the 100-meter dash and the 400-meter relay.

_____ 8. Hitler's early departure was a snub at Owens, but Jesse did not care.

_____ 9. Owens returned to the United States, he engaged in numerous exhibitions, including racing against a horse.

_____   10. In his later years Owens became an official
for the U.S. Olympic Committee, he never
received the recognition that many contemporary athletes do.

Exercise 8 Correcting Comma Splices and Run-Ons

*Identify each word group as a comma splice (CS), a run-on (RO), or
a complete sentence (OK), and correct the errors by making a dependent clause.*

_____   1. Roberto Clemente grew up poor in Puerto
Rico, he would become rich and famous.

_____   2. As a child he was determined to play baseball he used a tree limb to slug an old tennis
ball wrapped with yarn.

_____   3. Clemente excelled in youth and sandlot
teams, he signed a contract to play professional baseball.

_____   4. He played for the Pittsburgh Pirates between
1955 and 1972, he was once selected the
Most Valuable Player and twice had the
highest hitting average in the National
League.

_____   5. Often regarded as the best right fielder of all
time, he won twelve Gold Gloves for his de-
fensive play, and it was said he could throw
out runners from his knees.

_____   6. Clemente said that he was taught good val-
ues by his family and that he respected the
poor because they had learned about life
from their suffering.

_____   7. Clemente became wealthy, he always found
time to help the less fortunate.

_____   8. He liked to take an active part in his humanitarian work, in 1972 he decided to fly on an
airplane he had chartered to take supplies to
earthquake victims in Nicaragua.

_____ 9. The airplane crashed all aboard were killed.

_____ 10. He was a great baseball player and a great
human being many schools and parks have
been named after him.

Use a Semicolon

INCORRECT   The weather was disappointing, we canceled
the picnic.

CORRECT   The weather was disappointing; we canceled
the picnic.

CORRECT   The weather was disappointing; *therefore,* we
canceled the picnic.

This comma splice was corrected by a semicolon. The first correct
example shows the semicolon alone. The second correct example
shows a semicolon followed by the conjunctive adverb *therefore*
and a comma. The conjunctive adverb is optional, but, as we have
already seen, conjunctive adverbs can make the relationship between independent clauses stronger. Here is the list of conjunctive
adverbs you saw in Chapter 4.

however	on the other hand
otherwise	then
therefore	consequently
similarly	also
hence	thus

Recall the acronym HOTSHOT CAT, made up of the first letter of
each of these common conjunctive adverbs. The acronym will help
you remember them. Other conjunctive adverbs include *in fact, for
example, moreover, nevertheless, furthermore, now,* and *soon.*

Exercise 9 Correcting Comma Splices and Run-Ons

*Identify each word group as a comma splice (CS), a run-on (RO), or
a complete sentence (OK). Make corrections with a semicolon, and
add a conjunctive adverb if appropriate.*

_____ 1. Harry Houdini is often referred to as a magi-
cian, he was more famous as an escapologist.

_____ 2. He initially performed card tricks and other
common routines of illusion, he developed
some special nonescape acts.

_____ 3. One of his spectacular nonescape acts was making an elephant and its trainer disappear they were actually lowered into an empty swimming pool under the stage.

_____ 4. Soon Houdini grew bored with conventional magic, and he perfected some escape tricks.

_____ 5. Houdini learned to swallow and then regurgitate keys and tools, he could break free from restraints under water.

_____ 6. Houdini could also dislocate both shoulders at will he could escape easily from a straitjacket.

_____ 7. Houdini's most famous trick involved the Chinese Water Torture Cell, a steel and glass water-filled box in which he was chained and suspended upside down.

_____ 8. As an active member of a group of skeptics, he exposed spiritualists who claimed to contact the dead.

_____ 9. He decided to put his beliefs to a test, shortly before his death, he gave his wife a secret code and told her he would try to contact her from the grave.

_____ 10. Each Halloween night for a decade after he died, his wife and friends met and waited for a signal from Houdini, she gave up, saying, "Ten years is long enough to wait for any man."

Make Each Clause a Separate Sentence

INCORRECT   The weather was disappointing, we canceled the picnic.

CORRECT   The weather was disappointing. We canceled the picnic.

To correct the comma splice, replace the comma with a period, and begin the second sentence (the second independent clause) with a capital letter. This method is at once the simplest and most common method of correcting comma splices and run-ons. For a run-on,

insert a period between the two independent clauses and begin the
second sentence with a capital letter.

Exercise 10 Correcting Comma Splices and Run-Ons

*Identify each word group as a comma splice (CS), a run-on (RO), or
a complete sentence (OK). Correct the errors with a period and a
capital letter.*

    _____ 1. The world's fastest steel track roller coaster
is the Top Thrill Dragster it's at the Cedar
Point Amusement Park in Ohio.

    _____ 2. Riders rocket out of a starting gate they reach
a speed of 120 miles per hour in four seconds.

    _____ 3. The second-fastest roller coaster is in Japan
it goes a mere 106.8 miles per hour.

    _____ 4. Wooden roller coasters are downright pokey
in comparison the fastest reaches speeds of
only 78.3 miles per hour.

    _____ 5. If you're looking for the biggest drop, the
Top Thrill Dragster has that distinction, too.

    _____ 6. The largest drop on the Top Thrill Dragster
is 400 feet, compare that to the largest drop
on a wooden coaster, which is only 214 feet.

    _____ 7. The longest roller coaster ride of them all is
the Steel Dragon 2000 in Japan that coaster
is 8,133 feet long.

    _____ 8. You want the steepest angle of descent you
can choose from several steel track coasters
that allow you to plummet downward at a
90-degree angle.

    _____ 9. The steepest wooden coasters average about
55 degrees as a matter of fact, the steepest of
all is only 61 degrees.

    _____ 10. Most of the world's record-setting roller
coasters were opened between 2000 and
2003 thrill-seekers hope they'll continue to
get faster and steeper.

〜 Chapter Review

Exercise 11 Correcting Fragments, Comma Splices, and Run-Ons

Identify each word group as a comma splice (CS), a run-on (RO), a fragment (FRAG), or a complete sentence (OK). Correct the faulty sentences.

OK	correct
CS	comma splice
RO	run-on
FRAG	fragment

_____ 1. Piranhas live in freshwater streams and rivers of South America, they travel through the water in groups.

_____ 2. These ferocious-looking fish have a protruding lower jaw revealing a mouthful of sharp teeth.

_____ 3. Piranhas are meat-eaters they will eat just about any live or dead creature.

_____ 4. A school of piranhas consuming an animal the size of a pig in just minutes.

_____ 5. Like sharks, they are drawn toward the scent of blood in the water, movements such as splashing attract them, too.

_____ 6. When a school of piranhas is in a feeding frenzy.

_____ 7. The water appears to boil and become red with blood.

_____ 8. The piranha owes its savage reputation, in part, to adventurer Theodore Roosevelt.

_____ 9. Who wrote in a 1914 book that these ruthless predators would "devour alive any man or beast."

_____ 10. Roosevelt had heard of a man who went out alone on a mule, the mule returned to camp without its rider.

_____ 11. The man's skeleton was found in the water every bit of flesh had been stripped from his bones.

_____ 12. Still, Americans intrigued by stories bought piranhas for aquarium pets.

_____ 13. Fascinated by the fish's grisly reputation.

_____ 14. Perhaps admiring the silver body and bright red belly of this handsome creature.

_____ 15. As aquarium owners realized that their pets could be quite aggressive and dangerous.

_____ 16. Piranhas dumped into ponds, lakes, and reservoirs across the United States.

_____ 17. Fortunately, most of the waters were too cold for the piranhas to survive.

_____ 18. Truthfully, though, piranhas rarely attack humans, South Americans even bathe in piranha-infested waters.

_____ 19. South Americans also think piranhas are tasty and like to net, cook, and eat them.

_____ 20. However, U.S. officials are taking no chances, piranhas are illegal in many states.

Exercise 12 Correcting Fragments, Comma Splices, and Run-Ons

Correct each fragment, comma splice, and run-on. Choose whichever method of correction works best for each sentence problem.

Deserts are often referred to as wastelands. It is true that not as many plants grow there as grow in temperate zones, it is also true that animals do not live there in great numbers. But many plants and animals live and do quite well in the desert. Because of their adaptations.

Not all deserts have the same appearance. Many people think of the desert as a hot, sandy area. Actually sand covers only about 20 percent of the desert. Some deserts have mountains some others have snow.

Because deserts are dry for most of the year. Plants must conserve and store water. Several kinds of cacti can shrink during a dry season and swell during a rainy season. Some shrubs simply drop their leaves and use their green bark to manufacture chlorophyll. Seeds sometimes lying in the desert for several years before sprouting to take advantage of a rainfall.

Animals have quite effectively adjusted to the desert, some animals obtain moisture from the food they eat and require no water. One animal of the desert, the camel, produces fat. Which it stores in its hump. The fat allows the camel to reserve more body heat it needs little water. Still other animals feed only at night or are inactive for weeks or even months.

About 15 percent of the land of the earth is covered by deserts. That area increasing every year. Because of overgrazing by livestock. Also because of the destruction of forests. Areas that were once green and fertile will now support little life and only a small population of human beings.

6

Balancing Sentence Parts

We are surrounded by balance. Watch a colorful cross-frame, or diamond, kite as it soars in the sky. If you draw an imaginary line from the top to the bottom of the kite, you will see corresponding parts on either side. If you were to replace one of the sides with a loose-flapping fabric, the kite would never fly. A similar lack of balance can also cause a sentence to crash.

Consider these statements:

> "*To be* or not *to be*—that is the question." (dash added)

This line from *Hamlet,* by William Shakespeare, is one of the most famous in literature. Compare it to the well-balanced kite in a strong wind. Its parts are parallel and it "flies" well.

> "*To be* or *not being*—that is the question."

This line still vaguely resembles the sleek kite, but now the second phrase causes it to dip like an unbalanced kite. Lurching, the line begins to lose altitude.

> "*To be* or *death is the other alternative*—that is the question."

The line slams to the floor. Words scatter across the carpet. We go back to the revision board.

The first sentence is forceful and easy to read. The second is more difficult to follow. The third is almost impossible to understand. We understand it only because we know what it should look like from having read the original. The point is that perceptive readers are as critical of sentences as kite-watchers are of kites.

⌒ Basic Principles of Parallelism

Parallelism as it relates to sentence structure is usually achieved by joining words with similar words: nouns with nouns, adjectives (words that can describe nouns) with adjectives, adverbs (words that can describe verbs) with adverbs, and so forth.

79

Men, women, and *children* enjoy the show. (nouns)

The players are *excited, eager,* and *enthusiastic.* (adjectives)

The author wrote *skillfully* and *quickly.* (adverbs)

Parallel structure may also be achieved by joining groups of words with other similar groups of words: prepositional phrase with prepositional phrase, clause with clause, sentence with sentence.

She fell *in love* and *out of love* in a few minutes. (prepositional phrases)

Who he was and *where he came from* did not matter. (clauses)

He came in a hurry. He left in a hurry. (sentences)

Parallelism means balancing one structure with another of the same kind. Faulty parallel structure is awkward and draws unfavorable attention to what is being said.

NONPARALLEL   Pau Gasol's reputation is based on his ability in *passing, shooting,* and *he is good at rebounds.*

PARALLEL   Pau Gasol's reputation is based on his ability in *passing, shooting,* and *rebounding.*

In the first example, the words *passing* and *shooting* are of the same kind (verblike words used as nouns), but the rest of the sentence is different. You don't have to know terms to realize that there is a problem in smoothness and emphasis. Just read the material aloud. Then compare it with the parallel statement; *he is good at rebounds* is changed to *rebounding* to make a sentence that's easy on the eye and ear.

◠ Signal Words

Some words signal parallel structure. If you use *and,* the items joined by *and* should almost always be parallel. If they aren't, then *and* is probably inappropriate.

The weather is hot *and* humid. (*and* joins adjectives)

The car *and* the trailer are parked in front of the house. (*and* joins nouns)

The same principle is true for *but,* although it implies a direct contrast. Where contrasts are being drawn, parallel structure is essential to clarify those contrasts.

Ming *purchased* a Dodger Dog, *but* I *chose* the Stadium Peanuts. (*but* joins contrasting clauses)

Kachina *made* an A in math *but failed* her art class. (*but* joins contrasting verbs)

You should regard all the coordinating conjunctions (FAN-BOYS) as signals for parallel structure.

Exercise 1 Identifying Signal Words and Parallel Elements

Underline the parallel elements—words, phrases, or clauses—and circle the signal words in the following sentences. The words and phrases within parentheses are movie titles.

1. An old granny tells tales of wolves and children of the night.

   (*The Company of Wolves*)

2. Several convicts from another planet escape and fly to the planet Earth. (*Critters*)

3. Krite eggs hatch bloodthirsty babies and the babies continue the family tradition. (*Critters 2*)

4. Four people become trapped in a shopping mall with walking flesh-eaters and a gang of motorcyclists. (*Dawn of the Dead*)

5. A mad scientist dreams of creating life and using his ingenious talents. (*Frankenstein*)

6. He succeeds in producing a monster with the brain of a fiend, the emotions of a child, and the body of a giant.

7. Combining fact, fiction, and horror, this film is an imaginative tale of fear. (*Gothic*)

8. A man flees a disturbed past while being pursued by a lawman, a psychopathic killer, and the woman who still loves him. (*Night Breed*)

9. A man wants money he didn't earn, a sightless woman wants to see, and a man's past catches up with him. (*Night Gallery*)

10. Norman Bates attempts to put his life together and to put his old habits behind him. (*Psycho III*)

～ Combination Signal Words

The words *and* and *but* are the most common individual signal words used with parallel constructions. Sometimes, however, **combination words** signal the need for parallelism or balance. The most common ones are *either/or, neither/nor, not only/but also, both/and,* and *whether/or.* Now consider the following faulty sentences and two types of corrections:

> NONPARALLEL   *Either* we will win this game, *or* let's go out fighting.

> PARALLEL   *Either we will* win this game, *or we will* go out fighting.

The correction is made by changing *let's* to *we will* to parallel the *we will* in the first part of the sentence. The same construction should follow the *either* and the *or.*

> NONPARALLEL   Flour is used *not only* to bake cakes *but also* in paste.

> PARALLEL   Flour is used *not only to bake* cakes *but also to make* paste.

The correction is made by changing *in* (a preposition) to *to make* (an infinitive). Now an infinitive follows both *not only* and *but also.*

Exercise 2 Identifying Combination Signal Words and Parallel Elements

Underline the parallel elements—words, phrases, or clauses—and circle the combination signal words in the following sentences.

1. Robin Hood not only robbed from the rich but also gave to the poor. (*Adventures of Robin Hood*, 1938)

2. Both Humphrey Bogart and Katharine Hepburn star in this movie about two unlikely people traveling together through the jungle rivers of Africa during World War I. (*The African Queen*)

3. Dr. Jekyll discovers a potion, and now he can be either himself or Mr. Hyde. (*Dr. Jekyll and Mr. Hyde*)

4. An Oklahoma family moves to California and finds neither good jobs nor compassion in the "promised land." (*The Grapes of Wrath*)

5. In this Christmas classic, Jimmy Stewart stars as a man who can either die by suicide or go back to see what life would have been like without him. (*It's a Wonderful Life*)

6. During the Korean War, army surgeons discover that they must either develop a lunatic lifestyle or go crazy. (*M*A*S*H*)

7. An advertising executive not only gets tied up with an obnoxious and boring salesman but also goes with him on a wacky chase across the country. (*Planes, Trains, and Automobiles*)

8. In this flawless integration of animation and live action, Roger and Eddie try to discover both who framed Roger and who is playing patty-cake with his wife. (*Who Framed Roger Rabbit?*)

9. A long-suffering black woman named Celie experiences not only heartaches but also some joy as she rises from tragedy to personal triumph. (*The Color Purple*)

10. An independent man learns that he is expected to give up either his dignity or his life. (*Cool Hand Luke*)

⌢ Chapter Review

Exercise 3 Completing Sentences with Parallel Elements

Complete each of the following sentences by adding a word, phrase, or clause that is parallel to the italicized word, phrase, or clause.

1. We went to the zoo not only for *fun* but also for _____

   _____

2. He attended Utah State University for *a good education* and ___

   _____

3. For a college major, she was considering *English, history,* and ___

   _____

4. Mr. Ramos was a *good neighbor* and _____

   _____

5. My diet for breakfast that week consisted of *a slice of bread, a glass of low-fat milk,* and _____

   _____

6. She decided that she must choose between *a social life* and ____

_____

7. Either *she would make the choice,* or _____

_____

8. Because we are mutually supportive, either *we will all have a*

good time, or _____

_____

9. Like the Three Musketeers, our motto is "*All for one,* and ____

_____

10. My intention was to *work a year, save my money,* and _____

_____

Exercise 4 Writing Sentences with Parallel Elements

Use each of the following signal words or combined signal words in a sentence of eight or more words about the topic food.

1. and _____

_____

2. but _____

_____

3. so _____

_____

4. either/or _____

_____

5. both/and _____

_____

7

Verbs

This chapter covers the use of standard verbs. To some, the word *standard* implies "correct." A more precise meaning is "that which is conventional among educated people." Therefore, a standard verb is the right choice in most school assignments, most published writing, and most important public-speaking situations. However, we all change our language when we move from formal occasions to informal ones: we don't talk to our families in the same way we would speak at a large gathering in public; we don't text or email friends the same way we write a history report. But even with informal language we seldom change from standard to nonstandard usage.

∼ Regular and Irregular Verbs

Verbs can be divided into two categories, called *regular* and *irregular*. Regular verbs are predictable, but irregular verbs—as the term suggests—follow no definite pattern.

Verbs always show time. Present tense verbs show an action or a state of being that is occurring at the present time: I *like* your hat. Mike *is* at a hockey game right now. Present tense verbs can also imply a continuation from the past into the future: Carmen *drives* to work every day.

Past tense verbs show an action or a state of being that occurred in the past: We *walked* to town yesterday. Bao *was* president of the club last year.

Regular Verbs

Present Tense

For *he*, *she*, and *it*, regular verbs in the present tense add an -*s* or an -*es* to the base word. The following chart shows the present tense of the base word *ask*, which is a regular verb.

86

	Singular	Plural
FIRST PERSON	I ask	we ask
SECOND PERSON	you ask	you ask
THIRD PERSON	he, she, it asks	they ask

If the verb ends in -y, you might have to drop the -y and add -ies for he, she, and it.

	Singular	Plural
FIRST PERSON	I try	we try
SECOND PERSON	you try	you try
THIRD PERSON	he, she, it tries	they try

Past Tense

For regular verbs in the past tense, add -ed to the base form:

Base Form (Present)	Past
walk	walked
answer	answered

If the base form already ends in -e, add just -d:

Base Form (Present)	Past
smile	smiled
decide	decided

If the base form ends in a consonant followed by -y, drop the -y and add -ied.

Base Form (Present)	Past
fry	fried
amplify	amplified

Regardless of how you form the past tense, regular verbs in the past tense do not change forms. The following chart shows the past tense of the base word *like*, which is a regular verb.

	Singular	Plural
FIRST PERSON	I liked	we liked
SECOND PERSON	you liked	you liked
THIRD PERSON	he, she, it liked	they liked

Past Participles

The past participle uses the helping verbs *has, have,* or *had* along with the past tense of the verb. For regular verbs, the past participle form of the verb is the same as the past tense.

Base Form	Past	Past Participle
happen	happened	happened
hope	hoped	hoped
cry	cried	cried

Following is a list of some common regular verbs, showing the base form, the past tense, and the past participle. The base form can also be used with such helping verbs as *can, could, do, does, did, may, might, must, shall, should, will,* and *would.*

Regular Verbs

Base Form (Present)	Past	Past Participle
ask	asked	asked
answer	answered	answered
cry	cried	cried
decide	decided	decided
dive	dived (dove)	dived
drag	dragged	dragged
finish	finished	finished
happen	happened	happened
learn	learned	learned
like	liked	liked
love	loved	loved
need	needed	needed
open	opened	opened
start	started	started
suppose	supposed	supposed
walk	walked	walked
want	wanted	wanted

Irregular Verbs

Irregular verbs do not follow any definite pattern.

Base Form (Present)	Past	Past Participle
shake	shook	shaken
make	made	made
begin	began	begun

Some irregular verbs that sound similar in the present tense don't follow the same pattern.

Base Form (Present)	Past	Past Participle
ring	rang	rung
swing	swung	swung
bring	brought	brought

Present Tense

For *he, she,* and *it,* irregular verbs in the present tense add an *-s* or an *-es* to the base word. The following chart shows the present tense of the base word *break,* which is an irregular verb.

	Singular	Plural
FIRST PERSON	I break	we break
SECOND PERSON	you break	you break
THIRD PERSON	he, she, it breaks	they break

If the irregular verb ends in *-y,* you might have to drop the *-y* and add *-ies* for *he, she,* and *it.*

	Singular	Plural
FIRST PERSON	I fly	we fly
SECOND PERSON	you fly	you fly
THIRD PERSON	he, she, it flies	they fly

Past Tense

Like past tense regular verbs, past tense irregular verbs do not change their forms. The following chart shows the past tense of the irregular verb *do.*

	Singular	Plural
FIRST PERSON	I did	we did
SECOND PERSON	you did	you did
THIRD PERSON	he, she, it did	they did

Past Participles

Following is a list of some common irregular verbs, showing the base form (present), the past tense, and the past participle. Like regular verbs, the base forms can be used with such helping verbs as *can, could, do, does, did, may, might, must, shall, should, will,* and *would*.

Irregular Verbs

Base Form (Present)	Past	Past Participle
arise	arose	arisen
awake	awoke (awaked)	awaked
be	was, were	been
become	became	become
begin	began	begun
bend	bent	bent
blow	blew	blown
break	broke	broken
bring	brought	brought
buy	bought	bought
catch	caught	caught
choose	chose	chosen
cling	clung	clung
come	came	come
creep	crept	crept
deal	dealt	dealt
do	did	done
drink	drank	drunk
drive	drove	driven
eat	ate	eaten
feel	felt	felt
fight	fought	fought
fling	flung	flung
fly	flew	flown
forget	forgot	forgotten
freeze	froze	frozen
get	got	got (gotten)
go	went	gone
grow	grew	grown
have	had	had
know	knew	known
lead	led	led
leave	left	left
lose	lost	lost
mean	meant	meant

(continued)

Base Form (Present)	Past	Past Participle
read	read	read
ride	rode	ridden
ring	rang	rung
see	saw	seen
shine	shone	shone
shine	shined	shined
shoot	shot	shot
sing	sang	sung
sink	sank	sunk
sleep	slept	slept
slink	slunk	slunk
speak	spoke	spoken
spend	spent	spent
steal	stole	stolen
stink	stank (stunk)	stunk
sweep	swept	swept
swim	swam	swum
swing	swung	swung
take	took	taken
teach	taught	taught
tear	tore	torn
think	thought	thought
throw	threw	thrown
wake	woke (waked)	woken (waked)
weep	wept	wept
write	wrote	written

~ "Problem" Verbs

The following pairs of verbs are especially troublesome and confusing: *lie* and *lay*, *sit* and *set*, and *rise* and *raise*. One way to tell them apart is to remember which word in each pair takes a direct object. A direct object answers the question *whom* or *what* in connection with a verb. The words *lay*, *raise*, and *set* take a direct object.

He *raised* the window. (He *raised* what?)

Lie, *rise*, and *sit*, however, cannot take a direct object. We cannot say, for example, "He rose the window." In the following examples, the italicized words are objects.

Present Tense	Meaning	Past Tense	Past Participle	Example
lie	to rest	lay	lain	I lay down to rest.
lay	to place something	laid	laid	We laid the *books* on the table.
rise	to go up	rose	risen	The smoke rose quickly.
raise	to lift	raised	raised	She raised the *question*.
sit	to rest	sat	sat	He sat in the chair.
set	to place something	set	set	They set the *basket* on the floor.

～ The Twelve Verb Tenses at a Glance

Some languages, such as Chinese and Navajo, have no verb tenses to indicate time. English has a fairly complicated system of tenses, but most verbs pattern in what are known as the simple tenses: past, present, and future. Altogether there are twelve tenses in English. The following charts present those tenses in sentences, explain what the different tenses mean, and show how to form them.

Simple Tenses

PRESENT (may imply a continuation from past to future) I, we, you, they *drive.*   He, she, it *drives.*

PAST I, we, you, he, she, it, they *drove.*

FUTURE I, we, you, he, she, it, they *will drive.*

Perfect Tenses

PRESENT PERFECT (completed recently in the past; may continue into the present) I, we, you, they *have driven.*   He, she, it *has driven.*

PAST PERFECT (completed prior to a specific time in the past) I, we, you, he, she, it, they *had driven.*

FUTURE PERFECT   I, we, you, he, she, it, they *will have driven.*
(will occur at a time
prior to a specific
time in the future)

Progressive Tenses

PRESENT PROGRESSIVE   I *am driving.*
(in progress now)   He, she, it *is driving.*
You, they *are driving.*

PAST PROGRESSIVE   I, he, she, it *was driving.*
(in progress in the past)   You, they *were driving.*

FUTURE PROGRESSIVE   I, you, he, she, it, they *will be driving.*
(in progress in the future)

Perfect Progressive Tenses

PRESENT PERFECT PROGRESSIVE   I, you, they *have been driving.*
(in progress up to now)   He, she, it *has been driving.*

PAST PERFECT PROGRESSIVE   I, you, he, she, it, they *had been*
(in progress before another   *driving.*
event in the past)

FUTURE PERFECT PROGRESSIVE   I, you, he, she, it, they *will have*
(in progress before another   *been driving.*
event in the future)

⌒ Community Dialects and Standard Usage

Community dialects may be highly expressive and colorful. Popular songs and many television programs often use them well. Some people who use only a community dialect are much more gifted in communicating—explaining things, telling a story, getting to the point—than those who use only the standard dialect. And some people can use either the standard or the community dialect with equal skill. Those people are, in a limited sense, bilingual.

That said, we turn to our concern in this book: the standard use of language—and, specifically in this chapter, the standard use of verbs. Standard usage is advantageous because it is appropriate for the kind of writing and speaking you are likely to do in pursuing your college work and future career.

The following patterns will show the difference between a community dialect and the standard dialect for a regular verb (*walk*) and three irregular verbs (*do, be,* and *have*).

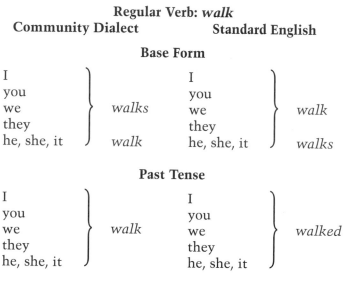

Regular Verb: *walk*

Community Dialect   **Standard English**

Base Form

Community Dialect		Standard English	
I you we they	*walks*	I you we they	*walk*
he, she, it	*walk*	he, she, it	*walks*

Past Tense

Community Dialect		Standard English	
I you we they he, she, it	*walk*	I you we they he, she, it	*walked*

Irregular Verb: *do*

Community Dialect   **Standard English**

Base Form

Community Dialect		Standard English	
I you we they	*does*	I you we they	*do*
he, she, it	*do*	he, she, it	*does*

Past Tense

Community Dialect		Standard English	
I you we they he, she, it	*done*	I you we they he, she, it	*did*

Irregular Verb: *be*

Community Dialect		Standard English	

Base Form

Community Dialect		Standard English	
I you we they he, she, it	*be, is,* or no verb	I	*am*
		you we they	*are*
		he, she, it	*is*

Past Tense

Community Dialect		Standard English	
I he, she, it we	*were*	I he, she, it	*was*
you they	*was*	we you they	*were*

Irregular Verb: *have*

Community Dialect		Standard English	

Base Form

Community Dialect		Standard English	
I you we they	*has*	I you we they	*have*
he, she, it	*have*	he, she, it	*has*

Past Tense

Community Dialect		Standard English	
I you we they he, she, it	*have* or *has*	I you we they he, she, it	*had*

Exercise 1 Selecting Verbs

Underline the standard English verb form.

1. I (talk, talks) fast at times. He (talk, talks) fast all the time.

2. I (talked, talks) to her on the phone. She (talked, talk) back.

3. We (talks, talked) about our secrets. We (talks, talked) softly.

4. We (walks, walked) home in the dark. I (walks, walked) in front.

5. I (walks, walk) fast when I am scared. She (walk, walks) fast all

   the time.

6. She (be, is) my best friend. I (be, am) her best friend.

7. We (be, is, are) very close. We (was, were) strangers last year.

8. At school, I (does, do) my work, and she (do, does) hers.

9. In the neighborhood, we (have, has) a close relationship. I (has,

   have) no need of other friends.

10. She (does, do) her schoolwork each day. I (does, do) mine

    almost every day.

Exercise 2 Selecting Verbs

Underline the standard English verb form.

1. This story is about Bill "Chick" Walker, who (lossed, lost) all

   he owned at the Wagon Wheel Saloon in Las Vegas.

2. Chick had (laid, layed) $1,000 on the red 21 at the roulette

   table.

3. For that spin, he (done, did) an amazing thing—he (won, wins).

4. But after a while, Chick (became, become) stupid, and his luck (ran, run) out.

5. Before he had (ate, eaten) breakfast, he accepted free drinks from the charming Trixie, who (served, serve) cocktails.

6. His judgment was soon (ruined, ruint) by the drinks, and he (put, putted) all his money on one spin.

7. That wager (cost, costed) Chick everything, and he couldn't (raise, rise) any more money.

8. Moreover, Trixie would not (sit, set) with him because she (like, liked) only winners.

9. Chick drained his glass, (rose, raised) from his red tufted vinyl barstool, and (head, headed) for the parking lot.

10. There he (known, knew) Bonnie Lou would be waiting for him because she (lust, lusted) for losers.

Exercise 3 Selecting Verbs

Underline the standard English verb form.

1. I wished I (stayed, had stayed) home.

2. I remembered that I (paid, had paid) him twice.

3. After parking their car, they (walk, walked) to the beach.

4. I (have, had) never encountered a genius until I met her.

5. I hoped that we (could have gone, went) to the big game.

6. They know that they (will complete, will have completed) the job before the first snow.

7. We (are considering, consider) the proposal.

8. He told us of the interesting life he (had led, led).

9. We went to the desert to see the cabin they (built, had built).

10. Tomorrow I (drive, will drive) to the supermarket for party items.

Exercise 4 Selecting Verbs

Underline the standard English verb form.

1. The scholars (worked, had worked) many hours before they solved the problem.

2. The shipping clerks wished they (had sent, sent) the package.

3. We (study, are studying) the issue now.

4. We (decide, will decide) on the winner tomorrow.

5. They reminded us that we (made, had made) the same promise before.

6. Before Teena went to Mexico, she (had never been, never was) out of the country.

7. Jake (had been napping, napped) when the alarm sounded.

8. By the time he finished talking, he realized that he (said, had said) too much.

9. At the end of the semester, the course grade (depends, will

   depend) on your ability to write well.

10. After he retired, I realized how much I (had learned, learned)

    from working with him.

Exercise 5 Selecting Verbs

Underline the standard English verb form.

1. According to legend, a vampire (lays, lies) in his coffin during

   the daylight hours.

2. Like a teenager, he (sets, sits) his own schedule: he sleeps all

   day and stays out all night.

3. He cannot (rise, raise) until after the sun sets.

4. Then the bloodsucker can (rise, raise) the coffin's lid and

   (set, sit) up.

5. He (rises, raises) from his bed hungry.

6. But don't bother (setting, sitting) a place for him at the

   dinner table.

7. He goes out hunting for victims who have unwisely

   (lain, laid) down their crucifixes, wooden stakes, and garlic

   necklaces.

8. He pounces quickly so that the victim has no time to (rise,

   raise) an alarm.

9. If he (lies, lays) his hands upon you, you're a goner.

10. But when the sun begins to (rise, raise) in the sky, this monster

must hurry back to bed to (lie, lay) his head down.

Exercise 6 Choosing Verb Tense

Underline the correct verb tense.

1. We (study, are studying) William Shakespeare's play *Romeo*

and Juliet.

2. The teenagers Romeo and Juliet (met, had met) at a party.

3. By the time the party was over, they (fell, had fallen) in love.

4. Unfortunately, though, their families (feud, were feuding), so

Romeo and Juliet (hid, had hidden) their affection for one

another.

5. They secretly (married, had married) and (planned, had

planned) to run away together.

6. But long before Juliet met Romeo, Juliet's father (decided, had

decided) that she would marry a man named Paris.

7. The night before her wedding, Juliet (took, had taken) a potion

that made her appear dead.

8. This tale (has, has had) a tragic ending because before Romeo

found Juliet in her tomb, he (was not informed, had not been

informed) that she wasn't really dead.

9. So he (committed, had committed) suicide, and Juliet (stabbed, had stabbed) herself when she awoke to find his body.

10. If I read this story again, I (have, will have) a tissue ready to dry my tears.

Exercise 7 Choosing Verb Tense

Underline the correct verb tense.

1. In the eighteenth century, Benjamin Franklin (is saying, said) that compound interest was the "eighth wonder of the world."

2. Today, taking advantage of compound interest (is, was) still one way to grow a fortune.

3. I wish I (had, had been) started investing years ago.

4. If I (will have, could have) saved $2,000 per year from age 21 on, I (would have, would have had) over a million dollars now.

5. I (have, had) never realized this until I did the math.

6. So I (have decided, could have been deciding) to begin investing money every month from now on.

7. Yesterday, I (determined, have determined) an amount I should save each week.

8. I hope that you (will have considered, are considering) doing the same thing.

9. By the time we're ready to retire, we (were, may be)

   millionaires.

10. Someday we (will worry, worried) about how to pay the bills.

Exercise 8 Using Verbs in Sentences

Use each of these words in a sentence of eight words or more.

1. *lie, lay* (rest), *lain, laid* _____

   _____

   _____

   _____

   _____

   _____

2. *sit, sat, set* _____

   _____

   _____

   _____

   _____

   _____

3. *is, was, were* _____

   _____

   _____

   _____

   _____

   _____

4. *do, does* (or *don't, doesn't*) _____

_____

_____

_____

_____

_____

〜 Subject-Verb Agreement

The basic principle of **subject-verb agreement** is that if the subject is singular, the verb should be singular, and if the subject is plural, the verb should be plural. There are ten major guidelines to ensure number agreement between subjects and verbs. In the examples under the following guidelines, the correct subjects and verbs are italicized.

1. Do not let words that come between the subject and verb affect agreement.

   - Modifying phrases and clauses frequently come between the subject and verb.

     The various *types* of drama *were* not *discussed.*

     Angela, who is hitting third, *is* the best player.

     The *price* of those shoes *is* too high.

   - Certain prepositions can cause trouble. The following words and phrases are prepositions, not conjunctions: *along with, as well as, besides, in addition to, including,* and *together with.* The words that function as objects of prepositions cannot also be subjects of the sentence.

     The *coach*, along with the players, *protests* the decision.

   - In compound subjects in which one subject is positive and one subject is negative, the verb agrees with the positive subject.

     Phillip, not the other boys, *was* the culprit.

2. Do not let inversions (verb before subject, not the normal order) affect the agreement of subject and verb.

   - Verbs and other words may come before the subject. Do not let them affect the agreement. To understand subject-verb relationships, recast the sentence in normal word order.

     Are Juan and his *sister* at home? (question form)

     Juan and his *sister are* at home. (normal order)

   - A sentence filler is a word that is grammatically independent of other words in the sentence. The most common fillers are *there* and *here*. Even though a sentence filler precedes the verb, it should not be treated as the subject.

     There *are* many *reasons* for his poor work. (The verb *are* agrees with the subject *reasons*.)

3. A singular verb agrees with a singular indefinite pronoun. (See page 128.)

   - Most indefinite pronouns are singular.

     Each of the women *is* ready at this time.

     Neither of the women *is* ready at this time.

     One of the children *is* not paying attention.

   - Certain indefinite pronouns do not clearly express either a singular or plural number. Agreement, therefore, depends on the meaning of the sentence. These pronouns are *all, any, none,* and *some*.

     All of the melon *was* good.

     All of the melons *were* good.

     None of the pie *is* acceptable.

     None of the pies *are* acceptable.

4. Two or more subjects joined by *and* usually take a plural verb.

     The *captain* and the *sailors were* happy to be ashore.

     The *trees* and *shrubs need* more care.

   - If the parts of a compound subject mean one and the same person or thing, the verb is singular; if the parts mean more than one, the verb is plural.

     The *secretary* and *treasurer is* not present. (one person)

The *secretary* and the *treasurer are* not present. (more than one person)

- When *each* or *every* modify singular subjects joined by *and*, the verb is singular.

    Each *boy* and each *girl brings* a donation.

    Each *woman* and *man has asked* the same questions.

5. Alternative subjects—that is, subjects joined by *or*, *nor*, *either/or*, *neither/nor*, *not only/but also*—should be handled in the following manner:

    - If the subjects are both singular, the verb is singular.

        Rosa or *Alicia* is responsible.

    - If the subjects are plural, the verb is plural.

        Neither the *students* nor the *teachers were* impressed by his comments.

    - If one of the subjects is singular and the other subject is plural, the verb agrees with the nearer subject.

        Either the Garcia *boys* or their *father goes* to the hospital each day.

        Either their *father* or the Garcia *boys go* to the hospital each day.

6. Collective nouns—*team, family, group, crew, gang, class, faculty,* and the like—take a singular verb if the group is considered a unit but a plural verb if the group is considered as a number of individuals.

    The *team is playing* well tonight.

    The *team are getting* dressed. (Here the individuals are acting not as a unit but separately. If you don't like the way this sounds, rewrite the sentence as "The members of the team are getting dressed.")

7. Titles of books, essays, short stories, and plays; a word spoken of as a word; and the names of businesses take a singular verb.

    The Canterbury Tales was written by Geoffrey Chaucer.

    Markle Brothers has a sale this week.

8. Sums of money, distances, and measurements are followed by a singular verb when a unit is meant. They are followed by a plural verb when the individual elements are considered separately.

    Three dollars was the price. (unit)

Three dollars were lying there. (individual)

Five years is a long time. (unit)

The *first five years were* difficult ones. (individual)

9. Be careful of agreement with nouns ending in *-s*. Several nouns ending in *-s* take a singular verb—for example, *aeronautics, civics, economics, ethics, measles, mumps.*

   Mumps is an extremely unpleasant disease.

   Economics is my major field of study.

10. Some nouns have only a plural form and so take only a plural verb—for example, *clothes, fireworks, scissors, pants,* and *glasses.*

    His *glasses are* dusty.

    Mary's *clothes were* stylish and expensive.

Exercise 9 Making Subjects and Verbs Agree

Underline the verb that agrees in number with the subject.

1. "Two Kinds" (is, are) a short story by Amy Tan.

2. My trousers (is, are) wrinkled.

3. Twenty pounds (is, are) a lot to lose in one month.

4. Physics (is, are) a difficult subject to master.

5. *60 Minutes* (is, are) a respected television program.

6. Sears (is, are) having a giant sale.

7. The scissors (is, are) very sharp.

8. Five miles (is, are) too far to walk.

9. The class (is, are) stretching their muscles.

10. My dog and my cat (is, are) sleeping on the couch.

Exercise 10 Making Subjects and Verbs Agree

Underline the verb that agrees in number with the subject.

1. Even after the devastation caused by Hurricane Katrina and then the oil spill, New Orleans (is, are) the site of one of the most celebrated parties in the United States.

2. Though at times the activities have been scaled back, Mardi Gras (is, are) an event that refuses to die.

3. Mardi Gras, which means "Fat Tuesday," (is, are) always forty-six days before Easter.

4. But twelve days before that, the crowd (begins, begin) to grow.

5. All of the bands in the state of Louisiana (converges, converge) on New Orleans.

6. A visitor, along with just about all of the city's residents, (enjoys, enjoy) nonstop jazz and blues music.

7. Cajun and Creole food (satisfies, satisfy) the revelers' hungry appetites.

8. There (is, are) numerous parades, but the best ones (occurs, occur) during the last five days of the celebration.

9. Each of the spectacular parade floats (is, are) decorated and (carries, carry) riders wearing costumes.

10. Four miles (is, are) the length of a typical parade route.

11. Beads, coins, cups, and an occasional medallion (is, are) tossed from the floats into the crowd.

12. People who line the parade route (tries, try) to catch as many trinkets as they can.

13. One float, the best of all of that parade's floats, (wins, win) an award.

14. Some of the most popular festivities, besides a good parade, (is, are) the masked balls.

15. Every one of the costumes (is, are) outrageous and unique.

16. *Cajun Mardi Gras Masks* (is, are) a book that will give you some ideas.

17. The celebration (is, are) a happening of fun and frenzy.

18. After dark, there (is, are) fireworks in the night sky.

19. Neither the participants nor the curious onlooker (wants, want) the party to end.

20. (Is, Are) these days of merrymaking something you'd enjoy?

⌢ Consistency in Tense

Consider this statement:

> We went (1) downtown, and then we watch (2) a movie. Later we met (3) some friends from school, and we all go (4) to the mall. For most of the evening, we play (5) video games in arcades. It was (6) a typical but rather uneventful summer day.

Does the shifting verb tense (to say nothing about the lack of development of ideas) bother you? It should! The writer makes several unnecessary changes. Verbs 1, 3, and 6 are in the past tense, and verbs 2, 4, and 5 are in the present tense. Changing all verbs to the past tense makes the statement much smoother.

> We went downtown, and then we watched a movie. Later we met some friends from school, and we all went to the mall. For most of the evening, we played video games in arcades. It was a typical but rather uneventful summer day.

In other instances you might want to maintain a consistent present tense. There are no inflexible rules about selecting a tense for a certain kind of writing, but you should be consistent, changing tense only for a good reason.

The present tense is customarily used in writing about literature, even if the literature was written long in the past:

> *Moby Dick* is a novel about Captain Ahab's obsession with a great white whale. Ahab *sets* sail with a full crew of sailors who *think* they *are going* on merely another whaling voyage. Most of the crew *are* experienced seamen.

The past tense is likely to serve you best in writing about your personal experiences and about historical events (although the present tense can often be used effectively to establish the feeling of intimacy and immediacy):

> In the summer of 1991, Hurricane Bob *hit* the Atlantic coast region. It *came* ashore near Cape Hatteras and *moved* north. The winds *reached* a speed of more than ninety miles per hour on Cape Cod but then *slackened* by the time Bob reached Maine.

Exercise 11 Making Verbs Consistent in Tense

Change the verbs in the following paragraph as necessary to maintain a mostly consistent past tense.

(1) Tarzan spoke to Jane in simple language. (2) His most famous words were "Me Tarzan, you Jane." (3) Before the arrival of Jane, there are only jungle friends for Tarzan. (4) Those animals

seldom used the full eight parts of speech. (5) For example, lions

seldom utter verbs. (6) Elephants had no patience with

prepositions. (7) Chimps condemn conjunctions. (8) Their

punctuation was replaced largely by snarls, growls, and breast-

beating. (9) Their language is well-suited to Tarzan. (10) To him,

jungle language was like swinging on a vine. (11) A one-syllable

yell is a full oration. (12) Jane never ridiculed his grammar or even

his yelling. (13) She holds back criticism of the king of the apes.

(14) Despite their difference in language skills, they establish hut

keeping. (15) They were very poor and wore simple garments made

of skins. (16) Their main transportation is well-placed hanging

vines. (17) Tarzan and Jane had a child. (18) They name him "Boy."

(19) Fortunately, they did not have another male child. (20) Such an

occurrence could have caused a language gridlock.

Exercise 12 Making Verbs Consistent in Tense

Change the verbs in the following paragraph as necessary to maintain a mostly consistent past tense.

(1) Once upon a time, a Professor Glen was very popular with

his students. (2) He kept long office hours and always speaks nicely

to his students on campus. (3) He even brought popcorn for them

to munch on during tests. (4) Respecting their sensitivity, he marks

with a soothing green ink instead of red. (5) He often told jokes and
listened attentively to their complaints about assignments. (6) The
leaders of student government elect him teacher of the century.
(7) Who would not admire such a person? (8) Then late one semester,
a strange and shocking thing happens. (9) Everywhere there were
students in despair. (10) Professor Glen no longer speaks openly to
students. (11) During his office hours, he locked his door and
posted a pit bull. (12) He corrects student papers in flaming scarlet.
(13) Instead of popcorn, he gave them hot scorn. (14) He told no
more jokes and sneered at their complaints about assignments.
(15) He sticks out his tongue at students on campus. (16) He offered
good grades for cash. (17) Professor Glen even accepts Visa cards
and validated parking. (18) One day the students heard a
thumping sound in a classroom closet. (19) Looking inside, they
find the true Professor Glen. (20) The other one was an evil twin
professor.

Exercise 13 Making Verbs Consistent in Tense

Correct verbs as needed in the following paragraph to achieve consistency in tense.

Guam is located in the Mariana chain of islands. It is first
inhabited by the Chamorro people. This island is a U.S. Trust

Territory since 1898, when the Spanish give up control after losing

the Spanish-American War. The Japanese occupy the island during

World War II until it is recaptured by the United States in July

1944. Today the island was a popular tourist spot for Asians as well

as being a site for several U.S. military bases. A beautiful tropical

island, Guam looked much like the Hawaiian Islands. The original

inhabitants come from Indonesia around 4,000 years ago. From

those times came the belief in Taotao Mona, spirits of the ancient

Chamorros; today most residents of Guam were Christian. People

born in Guam are American citizens. In fact, the motto of Guam

was "Where America's Day Begins."

◝◞ Active and Passive Voice

Which of these sentences sounds better to you?

>Andre Ethier slammed a home run.
>
>A home run was slammed by Andre Ethier.

Both sentences carry the same message, but the first expresses it
more effectively. The subject (*Andre Ethier*) is the actor. The verb
(*slammed*) is the action. The direct object (*home run*) is the receiver
of the action. The second sentence lacks the vitality of the first because the receiver of the action is the subject; the doer is embedded
in the prepositional phrase at the end of the sentence.

The first sentence demonstrates the active voice. It has an active verb (one that leads to a direct object), and the action moves
from the beginning to the end of the sentence. The second exhibits
the passive voice (with the action reflecting back on the subject).
When given a choice, you should usually select the active voice. It
promotes energy and directness.

The passive voice, though not usually the preferred form, does have its uses:

- When the doer of the action is unknown or unimportant

  My car was stolen. (The doer, a thief, is unknown.)

- When the receiver of the action is more important than the doer

  My neighbor was permanently disabled by an irresponsible drunk driver. (The neighbor's suffering, not the drunk driver, is the focus.)

As you can see, the passive construction places the doer at the end of a prepositional phrase (as in the second example) or does not include the doer in the statement at all (as in the first example). Instead, the passive voice places the receiver of the action in the subject position, and it presents the verb in its past tense form preceded by a *to be* helper. The transformation is a simple one:

| ACTIVE | Boris read the book. |
| PASSIVE | The book was read by Boris. |

Weak sentences often involve the unnecessary and ineffective use of the passive form.

Exercise 14 Using Active and Passive Voice

Rewrite these sentences to convert the verbs from passive to active voice.

1. A letter has been written by me to you.

2. An honest dollar was never made by his ancestors.

3. The assignment was approved by the instructor.

4. The instructor was given a much-deserved medal of valor by the president of the student body.

5. Few people noticed that most of the work was done by the quiet students.

6. The ballgame was interrupted by bats catching flies in the
   outfield.

7. The commotion at the apathy convention was caused by a
   person who attended.

8. The air was filled with speeches by him.

9. He doesn't have an enemy, but he is hated by all his friends.

10. His lips are never passed by a lie—he talks through his nose.

⁀ Strong Verbs

Because the verb is an extremely important part of any sentence, it
should be chosen with care. Some of the most widely used verbs are
the *being* verbs: *is, was, were, are, am.* We couldn't get along in
English without them, but writers often use them when more forceful and effective verbs are available.
   Consider these examples:

WEAK VERB	Regina *is* the leader of the race.
STRONG VERB	Regina *leads* in the race.
WEAK VERB	Regina *was* the first to finish.
STRONG VERB	Regina *finished* first.

Exercise 15 Using Strong Verbs

*Replace the weak verbs with stronger ones in the following sen-
tences. Delete unnecessary words to make each sentence even
more concise if you can.*

1. My watch is running slowly.

2. My computer is quite inexpensive.

3. The horse was a fast runner.

4. They were writers who wrote well.

5. The dog is sleeping on the bed.

6. Mr. Hawkins is a real estate salesperson.

7. José is in attendance at Santa Ana College.

8. This assignment is something I like.

9. We are the successful students here.

10. She is in the process of combing her hair.

Exercise 16 Using Strong Verbs

Replace the weak verbs with stronger ones in the following sentences. Delete unnecessary words to make each sentence even more concise if you can.

1. Babe Ruth was the hitter of many home runs.

2. The chef was a man with a fondness for food.

3. To graduate in two years is my plan.

4. John Hancock was the first signer of the Declaration of

   Independence.

5. Juanita is the organizer of the event.

6. Cooking is something she likes to do.

7. Veronica was the owner of the restaurant.

8. Venus Williams will be the winner of the tournament.

9. They were in love with each other.

10. His passion for her was in a state of demise.

◠ Chapter Review

Exercise 17 Correcting Verb Problems

Correct problems with verb form, tense, agreement, strength, and voice. As a summary of a novel, this piece should be mostly in the present tense.

Summary of *The Old Man and the Sea*

Santiago, one of many local fishermen, have not caught a fish

in eighty-four days. Young Manolin, despite the objections of his

parents, has a belief in the old man. His parents says Santiago is

unlucky, and they will not let their son go fishing with him.

The next day Santiago sit sail. Soon he catch a small

tuna, which he used for bait. Then a huge marlin hit the bait

with a strike. The old man cannot rise the fish to the surface,

and it pulled the boat throughout the rest of the day and during

the night.

During the second day, Santiago's hand is injured by the line

and he become extremely tired, but he holds on. When the fish

moves to the surface, Santiago notes that it was two feet longer

than his skiff. It is the biggest fish he has ever saw. He thinks in

wonder if he will be up to the task of catching it. With the line

braced across his shoulders, he sleeped for a while. As he dreams

gloriously of lions and porpoises and of being young, he is awaken by the fish breaking water again, and Santiago is sure the fish is tiring. He lays in the boat and waits.

On the third day, the fish came to the surface. Santiago pull steadily on the line, and finally it is harpooned and killed by Santiago. The fish is tied to the skiff by him. But sharks attacked and mutilate the huge marlin. Using an oar, he beats on the sharks courageously with all his strength, but they strips the fish to a skeleton.

With the bones still tied to the skiff, the exhausted old man returned to shore. Other fishermen and tourists marvel at the eighteen-foot skeleton of the fish as the old man lays asleep. The young boy knew he has much to learn from the old man and is determined to go fishing with him.

8

Pronouns

Should you say, "Between you and *I*" or "Between you and *me*"? What about "Let's you and *I* do this" or "Let's you and *me* do this"? Are you confused about when to use *who* and *whom*? Is it "Everyone should wear *their* coat," or "*his* coat," or "*his or her* coat"? Is there anything wrong with saying, "When *you* walk down the streets of Laredo"?

The examples in the first paragraph represent the most common problems people have with pronouns. This chapter will help you identify the standard forms and understand why they are correct. For you, the result should be expertise and confidence.

◠ Pronoun Case

Case is the form a pronoun takes as it fills a position in a sentence. Words such as *you* and *it* do not change, but others do, and they change in predictable ways. For example, *I* is a subject word and *me* is an object word. As you refer to yourself, you will select a pronoun that fits a certain part of sentence structure. You say, "*I* will write the paper," not "*Me* will write the paper," because *I* is in the subject position. But you say, "She will give the apple to *me*," not "She will give the apple to *I*" because *me* is in the object position. These are pronouns that do change:

Subject	Object
I	me
he	him
she	her
we	us
they	them
who	whom, whomever

118

Subjective Case

Person	Singular	Plural
First	I	we
Second	you	you
Third	he she it	they
	who	

Subjective pronouns can fill two positions in a sentence.

1. Pronouns in the subjective case may fill subject positions.

   a. Some subjective pronouns will be easy to identify because they are at the beginning of the sentence.

   I dance in the park.

   He dances in the park.

   She dances in the park.

   We dance in the park.

   They dance in the park.

   Who is dancing in the park?

   b. Others will be more difficult to identify because they are not at the beginning of a sentence and may not appear to be part of a clause. The words *than* and *as* are signals for these special arrangements, which can be called incompletely stated clauses.

   He is taller than *I* (am).

   She is younger than *we* (are).

   We work as hard as *they* (do).

   The words *am, are,* and *do,* which complete the clauses, have been omitted. We are actually saying, "He is taller than *I am,*" "She is younger than *we are,*" and "We work as hard as *they do.*" The italicized pronouns are subjects of "understood" verbs.

2. Pronouns in the subjective case may refer back to the subject.
   a. They may follow a form of the verb *to be,* such as *was, were, are, am,* and *is.*

   I believe it is *he.*

   It was *she* who spoke.

   The victims were *they.*

   b. Some nouns and pronouns refer back to an earlier noun without referring back through the verb.

   The leading candidates—Juan, Darnelle, Steve, Kimlieu, and *I*— made speeches.

Objective Case

Person	Singular	Plural
First	me	us
Second	you	you
Third	him her it	them
	whom	

Objective pronouns can also fill two positions in sentences.

1. Pronouns in the objective case may fill object positions.
   a. They may be objects after the verb. A direct object answers the question *What?* or *Whom?* in connection with the verb.

   We brought *it* to your house. (*What* did we bring? *it*)

   We saw *her* in the library. (*Whom* did we see? *her*)

   An indirect object answers the question *to whom* in connection with the verb.

   I gave *him* the message. (*To whom* did I give the message? *to him*)

   The doctor told *us* the test results. (*To whom* did the doctor tell the results? *to us*)

b. They may be objects after prepositions.

The problem was clear to *us*.

I offered the opportunity to Steve and *him*.

2. Object pronouns may also refer back to object words.

They gave the results to us—Judy and *me*.

The judge addressed the defendants—John and *her*.

Techniques for Determining Case

Here are three techniques that will help you decide which pronoun to use when the choice seems difficult:

1. If you have a compound element (such as a subject or an object of a preposition), consider only the pronoun part. The sound alone will probably tell you the answer.

   She gave the answer to Marie and (I, me).

   Marie and the pronoun make up a compound object of the preposition *to*. Disregard the noun, *Marie*, and ask yourself, "Would I say, 'She gave the answer *to me* or *to I*'?" The way the words sound would tell you the answer is *to me*. Of course, if you immediately notice that the pronoun is in an object position, you need not bother with sound.

2. If you are choosing between *who* (subject word) and *whom* (object word), look to the right to see if the next verb has a subject. If it does not, the pronoun probably is the subject, but if it does, the pronoun probably is an object.

   A related technique works the same way. If the next important word after *who* or *whom* in a statement is a noun or pronoun, the correct word will usually be *whom*. However, if the next important word is not a noun or pronoun, the correct word will be *who*.

   To apply these techniques, you must disregard qualifier clauses such as "I think," "it seems," and "we hope."

   The person (*who*, whom) works hardest will win. (*Who* is the correct answer because it is the subject of the verb *works*.)

   The person (who, *whom*) we admire most is José. (*Whom* is the correct answer because the next verb, *admire*, already has a subject, *we*. *Whom* is an object.)

Amanda is the person (*who*, whom), we hope, has won. (*We hope is a qualifier clause*, so we disregard it. Because we need a subject for the verb *has won*, we select the subject word *who*.)

3. *Let's* is made up of the words *let* and *us* and means "you *let us*"; therefore, when you select a pronoun to follow it, consider the two original words and select another object word—*me*.

Let's you and (I, *me*) take a trip to Westwood. (Think of "You let us, you and me, take a trip to Westwood." *Us* and *me* are object words.)

Exercise 1 Selecting Pronouns

Underline the correct pronouns.

1. (Who, Whom) did the judges crown Zucchini Queen?

2. To (who, whom) did the wealthy widow leave her vast fortune?

3. She was a woman (who, whom) loved cats, so her pets inherited her estate.

4. For (who, whom) are you buying this handsome set of Ginsu knives?

5. I know someone (who, whom) actually likes school cafeteria food.

6. (Who, Whom) is going to get the blue ribbon for the best pickles?

7. Seventeenth-century poet John Donne warned, "Ask not for (who, whom) the bell tolls; it tolls for thee."

8. How do I know (who, whom) to trust?

9. She addressed her love letter "To (Who, Whom) It May
   Concern."

10. The winner of the spelling bee was the child (who, whom)
    spelled the word *sesquipedalian* correctly.

Exercise 2   Selecting Pronouns

Underline the correct pronouns.

1. (She, Her) and (I, me) went to the Ripley's Believe It or Not
   Museum.

2. (We, Us) young people are fascinated by the weird, the gross,
   and the creepy.

3. I would rather go to the museum with you than with (she, her).

4. There are those (who, whom) would urge you not to waste your
   money to see oddities like shrunken heads and a portrait of
   John Wayne made of dryer lint.

5. Robert L. Ripley, an eccentric newspaper cartoonist (who,
   whom) loved to travel, collected strange things.

6. He is the man (who, whom) we can thank for acquiring many
   of the artifacts now housed in forty-four "Odditoriums" in ten
   different countries.

7. (Who, Whom) wouldn't be entertained by a stuffed six-legged
   cow or pictures of two-headed lambs and other freaks of nature?

8. And don't forget the bizarre videos, like the one of a man (who, whom) swallows and then regurgitates a live mouse.

9. I feel sorry for (whoever, whomever) misses the replica of the "Mona Lisa" made of croutons.

10. Just between you and (I, me), though, the wax figures of bizarre accident victims, like the man impaled on a crowbar, were a little unnerving.

Exercise 3 Selecting Pronouns

Underline the correct pronouns.

1. Let's you and (I, me) consider some stories called urban legends.

2. These are stories heard by people like you and (I, me), which are passed on as if they were true.

3. We hear them from people (who, whom) have heard them from others.

4. You have probably heard more of them than (I, me), but I'll tell some anyway.

5. One is about a guard dog named Gork (who, whom) was found choking in his owner's bedroom.

6. The owner, (who, whom) loved Gork dearly, took him to the veterinarian, left him, and headed home.

7. While driving home, the owner answered his cell phone, asking "To (who, whom) am I speaking?"

8. "This is your vet calling. Just between you and (I, me), you have a big problem here."

9. "Gork has someone's detached finger stuck in his throat, and I've called the police, (who, whom) are on their way to your house."

10. Eventually the police arrested an angry armed man (who, whom) they suspected had broken into the owner's house, where Gork had bitten off and choked on the intruder's finger while the intruder, (who, whom) had crawled into a closet, passed out from loss of blood.

Exercise 4 Selecting Pronouns

Underline the correct pronouns.

1. Another famous urban legend, involving two motorists, was told to my sister and (me, I) years ago.

2. Between you and (I, me), the story is sexist, but this is the way (we, us) heard it.

3. A motorist, (who, whom) was named Al, needed someone to push his car, so he called on Sue, his neighbor, (who, whom) lived next door.

4. "I need a push to get my car started," he said to her. "Let's you and (I, me) work together, and I'll be grateful forever."

5. "You're a special person (who, whom) I've always wanted to befriend," she said happily. "Tell me what to do."

6. "My car has an automatic transmission, which means the car won't start at less than thirty-five miles per hour," said Al, (who, whom) talked fast.

7. Al sat in his car as happy as (her, she) when he looked in his rearview mirror and saw (she, her) heading toward his back bumper at a high speed.

8. After the collision, Al stumbled out of his car and confronted Sue, (who, whom), despite her injuries, was smiling.

9. "Look what you've done to you and (I, me)!" Al yelled.

10. "Let's you and (I, me) review what you said," she answered coolly. "You said, 'thirty-five miles per hour,' and that's exactly what I was doing."

Pronoun-Antecedent Agreement

Every pronoun refers to an earlier noun, the **antecedent** of the pronoun, which is the noun that the pronoun replaces. The pronoun brings the reader back to the earlier thought. Here are some examples:

I tried to buy *tickets* for the concert, but *they* were all sold.

Roger painted a picture of a pickup truck. *It* was so good that *he* entered *it* in an art show.

A pronoun agrees with its antecedent in person, number, and gender. **Person**—first, second, or third—indicates perspective, or point of view. **Number** indicates singular or plural. **Gender** indicates sex: masculine, feminine, or neuter.

Subject Words			*Object Words*		
Person	Singular	Plural	**Person**	Singular	Plural
First	I	we	**First**	me	us
Second	you	you	**Second**	you	you
Third	he, she, it	they	**Third**	him, her, it	them

Agreement in Person

Avoid needless shifting in person, which means shifting of point of view, such as from *I* to *you*. The following paragraph is an example of an inconsistent point of view. See if you can tell where the shifts occur.

INCONSISTENT   The wedding did not go well. It was a disaster. *You* could see the trouble develop when the caterers started serving drinks before the ceremony. Then the bride started arguing with her future mother-in-law. *I* was ready to leave right away. After that, the sound system went out and the band canceled. *You* wished *you* hadn't come, but *you* had to stay. *I* will never forget that day.

The word *you* is second-person point of view; the word *I* is first person. When the writer switches back and forth, the result is reader confusion and annoyance. The following revision corrects the problem by making the point of view consistently first person.

CONSISTENT   The wedding did not go well. It was a disaster. *I* could see the trouble develop when the caterers started serving drinks before the ceremony. Then the bride started arguing with her future mother-in-law. *I* was ready to leave right away. After that, the sound system went out and the band canceled. *I* wished *I* hadn't come, but *I* had to stay. *I* will never forget that day.

Agreement in Number

Most problems with pronoun-antecedent agreement involve number. The principles are simple: If the antecedent (the word the pronoun refers back to) is singular, use a singular pronoun. If the antecedent is plural, use a plural pronoun.

1. A singular antecedent requires a singular pronoun.

   Riley forgot *his* notebook.

2. A plural antecedent requires a plural pronoun.

   Many *students* cast *their* votes today.

3. A singular indefinite pronoun as an antecedent takes a singular pronoun. Most indefinite pronouns are singular. The following are common indefinite singular pronouns: *anybody, anyone, each, either, everybody, everyone, no one, nobody, one, somebody, someone.*

   Each of the girls brought *her* book.

4. A plural indefinite pronoun as an antecedent takes a plural pronoun.

   Few knew *their* assignments.

5. Certain indefinite pronouns do not clearly express either a singular or plural number. Agreement, therefore, depends on the meaning of the sentence. These pronouns are *all, any, none,* and *some.*

   All of the melon *was* good.

   All of the melons *were* good.

   None of the pie *is* acceptable.

   None of the pies *are* acceptable.

6. Two or more antecedents, singular or plural, take a plural pronoun. Such antecedents are usually joined by *and* or by commas and *and.*

   Max and his *parents* bought *their* presents early.

   The *players, team owner,* and *fans* expressed *their* views.

7. Alternate antecedents—that is, antecedents joined by *or, nor, whether/or, either/or, neither/nor, not only/but also*—require a pronoun that agrees with the nearer antecedent.

> Neither Igor nor his *friends* lost *their* way.
>
> Neither his friends nor *Igor* lost *his* way.

8. In a sentence with the expression *one of*, the antecedent is usually the plural noun that follows.

> He is one of those *people who* want *their* money now.

9. In a sentence with the expression *only one of*, the antecedent is usually the singular word *one*.

> Alexandra is the *only one of* the members *who* wants *her* money now.

10. When collective nouns such as *team, jury, committee,* and *band* are used as antecedents, they take a singular pronoun if they are considered as units.

> The *jury* is doing *its* [not *their*] best.

When individual behavior is suggested, collective nouns take a plural form.

> The *jury* are putting on *their* coats.

11. The words *each, every,* and *many a(n)* before a noun make the noun singular.

> *Each child* and *adult* was *his* or *her* own authority.
>
> *Each* and *every person* doubted *himself* or *herself*.
>
> *Many a* person is capable of knowing *himself* or *herself*.

Agreement in Gender

The pronoun should agree with its antecedent in gender, if the gender of the antecedent is specific. Masculine and feminine pronouns are gender-specific: *he, him, she, her.* Others are neuter: *I, we, me, us, it, they, them, who, whom, that, which.* The words *who* and *whom* refer to people. *That* can refer to ideas, things, and people, but usually not to people. *Which* refers to ideas and things, but never to people.

> My *girlfriend* gave me *her* best advice. (feminine)
>
> Mighty *Casey* tried *his* best. (masculine)
>
> The *people with whom* I work are loud. (neuter)

Indefinite singular pronouns used as antecedents require, of course, singular pronouns. Handling the gender of these singular pronouns is not as obvious; opinion is divided.

1. Traditionally, writers have used the masculine form of pronouns to refer to the indefinite singular pronouns when the gender is unknown.

   Everyone should work until *he* drops.

2. The use of the masculine form of pronouns alone, however, suggests a sex bias. To avoid a perceived sex bias, most writers prefer to use *he or she* or *his or her* instead of just *he* or *his*.

   Everyone should work until *he or she* drops.

3. Although option 1 is less cumbersome, it is offensive and illogical to many listeners and readers, and option 2 used several times in a short passage can be awkward. To avoid those possible problems, writers often use plural forms.

   All people should work until *they* drop.

In any case, avoid using a plural pronoun with a singular indefinite pronoun; such usage violates the basic principle of number agreement.

INCORRECT   *Everyone* should do *their* best.

Exercise 5 Selecting Pronouns: Person, Gender, and Number

Correct the faulty pronouns for problems in person, gender, and number.

1. The person which founded Procrastinators International has

   never scheduled a meeting of members.

2. Everyone will now pause to offer their thanks to the person

   who invented the air conditioner.

3. The savvy airboat rider keeps their mouth closed to avoid

   eating bugs.

4. The individual which was abducted by aliens promises to tell

   all in her upcoming book.

5. People which live in stone houses should not throw glass.

6. Practically every person is bothered by their particular

   pet peeve.

7. Around these parts, the wooly worm is thought to predict the

   severity of the upcoming winter by the thickness of their coat.

8. In the summer, a cricket can reveal the temperature if you

   count the number of their chirps over fifteen seconds.

9. Someone which adds thirty-seven to the number of the

   cricket's chirps will know exactly how hot it is in degrees

   Fahrenheit.

10. So far, the only thing the cockroach has been able to reveal is

    the lack of success of the restaurant they call home.

Exercise 6 Selecting Pronouns: Person, Gender, and Number

Underline the correct pronoun for person, gender, and number.

1. The band always ends (its, their) concert with a lively

   tuba solo.

2. Every American should save money, or (they, he or she) may

   not have enough for retirement.

3. Each camper must bring (their, his or her) own shaving cream.

4. If the class doesn't go on the field trip, (it, they) will miss the

   mummy exhibit.

5. Each of those farmers knows that (he, they) must rotate (his,

   their) crops.

6. Pauline and Reggie left (their, his or her) hearts in San

   Francisco.

7. Everyone should leave (their, his or her) world a better place.

8. Neither the bride nor the bridesmaids could control (her, their)

   giggles during the ceremony.

9. He is one of those men who likes to drive (his, their) car fast.

10. Every rose has (its, their) thorn, every dog has (its, his or her)

    day, and every cloud has (its, his or her) silver lining.

〜 Pronoun Reference

A pronoun must refer clearly to its antecedent. Because a pronoun
is a substitute word, it can express meaning clearly and definitely
only if its antecedent is easily identified.

   In some sentence constructions, gender and number make the
reference clear.

> Cliff and Martina discussed *his* absences and *her* good atten-
> dance. (gender)
>
> If the three older boys in the *club* carry out those plans, *it* will
> break up. (number)

   Avoid ambiguous reference. The following sentences illustrate
the kind of confusion that results from structuring sentences with
more than one possible antecedent for the pronoun.

> UNCLEAR   Brady gave Owen *his* money and clothes.
>
> CLEAR   Brady gave his own money and clothes to Owen.
>
> UNCLEAR   Kylie told her sister that *her* car had a flat tire.
>
> CLEAR   Kylie said to her sister, "Your car has a flat tire."

When using a pronoun to refer to a general idea, make sure that the reference is clear. The pronouns used frequently in this way are *this*, *that*, *which*, and *it*. The best solution may be to recast the sentence to omit the pronoun in question.

UNCLEAR	Molly whistled the same tune over and over, *which* irritated me.
CLEAR	Molly whistled the same tune over and over, a *habit* that irritated me.
RECAST	Her whistling the same tune over and over irritated me.

Exercise 7 Selecting Pronouns: Reference and Agreement

Correct the problems in pronoun reference and agreement.

1. I eat fast food only three times a week, which is un-American of me.

2. The supervisors told the staff members that they would be getting a big raise.

3. If a woman is looking for quality men, you should log on to www.select-a-hunk.com.

4. Bridget called to find out the store's hours, but they didn't answer.

5. When he smashed into the pyramid of cat food with his shopping cart, it was destroyed.

6. It says in the newspaper that an elephant is on the loose.

7. I tend to submit my assignments late, which hurts my grade.

8. The Great Oz told the Tin Man that he already possessed the thing he craved most.

9. They say that the horse named Cheese Whiz may win the Triple Crown.

10. Spiderman told Superman that he may have given up on love too soon.

⌒ Chapter Review

Exercise 8 Writing Sentences with Correct Pronouns

Write a sentence using each of the following words. Do not use the word as the first one in the sentence. One sentence should contain the word between *before a pronoun, such as "Between you and _____,"and one sentence should contain the contraction* let's *before a pronoun, such as "Let's you and _____."*

1. she _____

_____

_____

2. her _____

_____

_____

3. him _____

_____

_____

4. us _____

_____

_____

5. who _____

_____

_____

6. whom _____

_____

_____

7. me _____

_____

_____

8. I _____

_____

_____

9. they _____

_____

_____

10. them _____

_____

_____

9

Adjectives and Adverbs

Adjectives modify (describe) nouns and pronouns and answer the questions *Which one? What kind?* and *How many?*

WHICH ONE?　The <u>new</u> <u>car</u> is mine.
　　　　　　　　adj　n

WHAT KIND?　<u>Mexican</u> <u>food</u> is my favorite.
　　　　　　　adj　　　n

HOW MANY?　A <u>few</u> <u>friends</u> are all one needs.
　　　　　　　adj　　n

Adverbs modify verbs, adjectives, or other adverbs and answer the questions *How? Where? When?* and *To what degree?* Most words ending in *-ly* are adverbs.

WHERE?　The cuckoo <u>flew</u> <u>south</u>.
　　　　　　　　　v　　adv

WHEN?　The cuckoo <u>flew</u> <u>yesterday</u>.
　　　　　　　　　v　　　adv

WHY?　The cuckoo <u>flew</u> <u>because of the cold weather</u>.
　　　　　　　　　v　　　　　　adv phrase

HOW?　The cuckoo <u>flew</u> <u>swiftly</u>.
　　　　　　　　　v　　　adv

<u>Without adjectives and adverbs</u>, <u>even</u> John Steinbeck, the *<u>famous</u>*
　　　adv phrase　　　　　　　adv　　　　　　　　　　　adj

<u>Nobel Prize–winning</u> author, <u>surely</u> could <u>not</u> have described the
　　　adj　　　　　　　　　　　adv　　　adv

<u>crafty</u> octopus <u>very</u> <u>well</u>.
　adj　　　　　adv　adv

136

Exercise 1 Using Adjectives and Adverbs

The following excerpt is from John Steinbeck's novel Cannery Row. Before you read the next paragraph, fill in the blanks for the adjectives and adverbs that have been omitted in this exercise.

(1) _____ the (2) _____ murderer, the octopus, steals

(3) _____, (4) _____, (5) _____, moving like a

(6) _____ mist, pretending (7) _____ to be a bit of weed,

(8) _____ a rock, (9) _____ a lump of (10) _____

meat while its (11) _____ eyes watch (12) _____. It

oozes and flows toward a (13) _____ crab, and as it comes close

its (14) _____ eyes burn and its body turns (15) _____

with the (16) _____ color of anticipation and rage. (17)

_____, (18) _____, it runs (19) _____ on the

tips of its arms, as (20) _____ as a (21) _____ cat. It

leaps (22) _____ on the crab, there is a puff of (23)

_____ fluid, and the (24) _____ mass is obscured

in the (25) _____ cloud while the octopus murders the crab.

Of course, Steinbeck vividly depicts his subject through his skillful choice of nouns such as *murderer* and *rage*, and of verbs such as *steals, oozes, flows, burn, runs,* and *leaps,* but the absence of adjectives and adverbs eliminates a whole dimension of expression. The missing adjectives and adverbs are the following: (1) Then, (2) creeping, (3) out, (4) slowly, (5) softly, (6) gray, (7) now, (8) now, (9) now, (10) decaying, (11) evil, (12) coldly, (13) feeding, (14) yellow, (15) rosy, (16) pulsing, (17) Then, (18) suddenly,

(19) lightly, (20) ferociously, (21) charging, (22) savagely, (23) black, (24) struggling, (25) sepia.

We have two concerns regarding the use of adjectives and adverbs in writing. One is a matter of diction, or word choice—in this case, how to select adjectives and adverbs that will strengthen the writing. The other is how to identify and correct problems with these modifiers.

~ Selecting Adjectives and Adverbs

If you want to finish the sentence "She danced _____," you have many adverbs to select from, including these:

bewitchingly	angelically	quaintly	zestfully
gracefully	grotesquely	carnally	smoothly
divinely	picturesquely	serenely	unevenly

If you want to finish the sentence "She was a(n) _____ speaker," you have another large selection, this time of adjectives such as the following:

distinguished	dependable	effective	sly
influential	impressive	polished	astute
adequate	boring	abrasive	humorous

Adjectives and adverbs can be used to enhance communication. If you have a thought, you know what it is, but when you deliver that thought to someone else, you may not say or write what you mean. Your thought may be eloquent and your word choice weak. Keep in mind that no two words mean exactly the same thing. Further, some words are vague or general. If you settle for a common word such as *good* or a slang word such as *neat* to characterize something that you like, you will be limiting your communication. Of course, those who know you best may understand fairly well; after all, certain people who are really close may be able to convey ideas using only grunts and gestures.

But what if you want to write to someone you hardly know to explain how you feel about an important issue? Then the more precise the word, the better the communication. By using modifiers you may be able to add significant information. Anything can be overdone, however, so use adjectives and adverbs wisely and economically.

Your first resource in searching for more effective adjectives should be your own vocabulary storehouse. Another resource is a good thesaurus (book of synonyms). Finally, you may want to collaborate with others to discuss and share ideas.

Exercise 2 Using Adjectives

Provide adjectives to modify these nouns, using a dictionary, a thesaurus, or the resources designated by your instructor. Use only single words, not adjective phrases.

1. A(n) _____ dog ignored the cat.

2. A(n) _____ comedian waited for applause.

3. A(n) _____ voice cried out in the night.

4. A(n) _____ neighbor turned up his boom box.

5. A(n) _____ ballplayer never gives up.

6. A(n) _____ party occurs only in one's imagination.

7. A(n) _____ singer sang off key.

8. A(n) _____ date waited at the club.

9. A(n) _____ car careened down the street.

10. A(n) ____ _____ job is hard to find.

Exercise 3 Using Adverbs

Provide adverbs to modify these verbs, using a dictionary, a thesaurus, or the resources designated by your instructor. Use only single words, not adverb phrases.

1. Write _____ and clearly.

2. Run _____ and get help.

3. Talk _____ and carry a big stick.

4. Walk _____ and think fast.

5. Marry _____ and suffer at leisure.

6. Smile _____ at your boss.

7. Drive _____ and carefully.

8. Leave _____ and forget my name.

9. Laugh _____ at adversity.

10. Study _____ and get smart.

Comparative and Superlative Forms

For making comparisons, most adjectives and adverbs have three different forms: the positive (one), the comparative (two), and the superlative (three or more).

Adjectives

1. Some adjectives follow a regular pattern:

Positive (one)	Comparative (two)	Superlative (three or more)
nice	nicer	nicest
rich	richer	richest
big	bigger	biggest
tall	taller	tallest
lonely	lonelier	loneliest
terrible	more terrible	most terrible
beautiful	more beautiful	most beautiful

These are usually the rules:

a. Add *-er* to short adjectives (one or two syllables) to rank units of two:

Julian is *nicer* than Sam.

b. Add *-est* to short adjectives (one or two syllables) to rank units of three or more:

Of the fifty people I know, Julian is the *kindest*.

c. Add the word *more* to long adjectives (three or more syllables) to rank units of two:

My hometown is *more beautiful* than yours.

d. Add the word *most* to long adjectives (three or more syllables) to rank units of three or more:

My hometown is the *most beautiful* in all America.

2. Some adjectives are irregular in the way they change to show comparison.

Positive (one)	Comparative (two)	Superlative (three or more)
good	better	best
bad	worse	worst

Adverbs

1. For most adverbs, use the word *more* before the comparative form (two) and the word *most* before the superlative form (three or more).

> Pedro performed *skillfully*. (modifier)
>
> Pedro performed *more skillfully* than Kari. (comparative modifier)
>
> But Lorena performed *most skillfully* of all. (superlative modifier)

2. Avoid double negatives. Words such as *no, not, none, nothing, never, hardly, barely,* and *scarcely* should not be combined.

> DOUBLE NEGATIVE   I do *not* have *no* time for recreation. (incorrect)
>
> SINGLE NEGATIVE   I have *no* time for recreation. (correct)
>
> DOUBLE NEGATIVE   I've *hardly never* lied. (incorrect)
>
> SINGLE NEGATIVE   I've *hardly* ever lied. (correct)

3. Do not confuse adjectives with adverbs. Among the most commonly confused adjectives and adverbs are *good/well, bad/badly,* and *real/really.* The words *good, bad,* and *real* are always adjectives. *Well* is sometimes an adjective. The words *badly* and *really* are always adverbs. *Well* is usually an adverb.

   To distinguish these words, consider what is being modified. Remember that adjectives modify nouns and pronouns and that adverbs modify verbs, adjectives, and other adverbs.

> WRONG   I feel *badly* today. (We're concerned with the condition of *I*.)
>
> RIGHT   I feel *bad* today. (The adjective *bad* modifies the pronoun *I*.)
>
> WRONG   Jasmine feels *well* about that choice. (We're concerned with the condition of *she*.)
>
> RIGHT   Jasmine feels *good* about that choice. (The adjective *good* modifies the pronoun *she*.)

WRONG   Wyatt plays the piano *good*. (The adjective *good* modifies
the verb *plays*, but adjectives should not modify verbs.)

RIGHT   Wyatt plays the piano *well*. (The adverb *well* modifies
the verb *plays*.)

WRONG   He did *real* well. (Here the adjective *real* modifies the
adverb *well*, but adjectives should not modify adverbs.)

RIGHT   He did *really* well. (The adverb *really* modifies the adverb *well*.)

4. Do not use an adverb such as *very, more*, or *most* before adjectives such as *perfect, round, unique, square*, and *straight*.

WRONG   It is more round.

RIGHT   It is round.

RIGHT   It is more nearly round.

Exercise 4   Selecting Adjectives and Adverbs

Underline the correct word or words.

1. Betty Skelton was one of the (most, more) successful female

   stunt pilots of the 1940s and 1950s.

2. In the 1930s and 1940s, the public was (real, really) interested

   in watching acrobatic air shows.

3. Skelton was (not hardly, hardly) going to sit there and watch

   the men have all the fun.

4. She wanted (bad, badly) to learn to fly, and she was (real, really)

   adventurous, so she learned to perform daredevil feats.

5. Her small, agile airplane, which was named Little Stinker,

   performed tricks (well, good).

6. One of her (better, best) stunts was the inverted ribbon cut.

7. It was a (real, really) thrill to watch her fly upside down twelve feet off the ground and use her propeller to slice a foil strip strung between two poles.

8. The crowd could (not hardly, hardly) contain its excitement.

9. She earned only $25 for each air show, so the pay was (bad, badly).

10. But according to Betty, her six-year acrobatic flying career was the (more, most) fun time in her life.

Exercise 5 Selecting Adjectives and Adverbs

Correct any problems with adjectives and adverbs in the following sentences.

1. After her eighth cup of coffee, she is one of the most liveliest women in the office.

2. Levi wanted the fry cook job real bad, but his interview didn't go good.

3. As Zeke strolled through Bronco Bob's Bar and Boot Shop, he knew that he had never seen a more perfect setting for a square dance.

4. Ryan was real sorry for eating her artistic masterpiece, so he offered his sincere apologies.

5. Of the two weightlifters, Carlos is best at clean-and-jerk lifts.

6. Sarah looks well in spandex and sequins.

7. After her divorce, Emily finally felt happily.

8. The skater fell during every one of her jumps, so she performed pretty bad.

9. My baby cries louder than that baby.

10. In a blind taste test, most consumers said that Squirt was the better of the three leading brands of imitation cheese food.

Exercise 6 Selecting Adjectives and Adverbs

Cross out the mistake in each sentence and write in the correction above it.

1. Ping-Sim thought his teacher had a most unique method of lecturing.

2. Some jobs are done easier by blind people than by those with sight.

3. It was up to the parents to decide if this kind of movie is real bad for children.

4. The adventure of life is too impossible to discuss.

5. Oscar felt badly about rejection slips but worse about his bank account.

6. Victor was not the stronger of the pair, but he was the best boxer.

7. The whole class thought Kyoka's sunglasses the most perfect they had seen.

8. The suspect became violenter as the police drew nearer.

9. Of all the potential winners, Miss Idaho was considered the more beautiful.

10. The United States has no central educational authority, but overall it does good.

11. An unambiguous word only can mean one thing.

12. It is real easy to forget that "liquor" used to mean "liquid."

13. Hurtful experiences in childhood don't fade out easy.

14. Katie said he had all ready ruined his reputation by making her buy her own flowers.

15. A trembling voice may indicate that the speaker does not feel alright.

16. Julian had two ways of starting a speech: one way was with a definition, but the easiest way was with a joke.

17. Sherman choked as if the very words tasted badly to him.

18. Natasha made a real good decision.

19. Erika didn't say the food was terrible; only she said it was bad.

20. On controversial topics, Garrett was all together too easily offended.

◯ Dangling and Misplaced Modifiers

Modifiers should clearly relate to the word or words they modify.

1. A modifier that gives information but doesn't refer to a word or group of words already in the sentence is called a **dangling modifier**.

   DANGLING *Walking down the street,* a snake startled him. (The modifier is not connected grammatically to a particular word.)

   CORRECT *Walking down the street,* Don was startled by a snake.

   CORRECT As *Don* walked down the street, *he* was startled by a snake.

   DANGLING *At the age of six,* my uncle died. (Who was six years old? The person isn't mentioned in the modifier.)

   CORRECT *When I was six,* my uncle died.

2. A modifier that is placed so that it modifies the wrong word or words is called a **misplaced modifier**. The term also applies to words that are positioned to unnecessarily divide closely related parts of sentences such as infinitives (*to* plus verb) or subjects and verbs.

   MISPLACED The sick man went to a doctor *with a high fever.*
   CORRECT The sick man *with a high fever* went to a doctor.
   MISPLACED I saw a great movie *sitting in my pickup.*
   CORRECT *Sitting in my pickup,* I saw a great movie.
   MISPLACED Kim found many new graves *walking through the cemetery.*
   CORRECT *Walking through the cemetery,* Kim found many new graves.
   MISPLACED I forgot all about my sick dog *kissing my girlfriend.*
   CORRECT *Kissing my girlfriend,* I forgot all about my sick dog.
   MISPLACED They tried to *earnestly and sincerely* complete the task. (splitting of the infinitive *to complete*)
   CORRECT They tried *earnestly and sincerely* to complete the task.

MISPLACED   My neighbor, *while walking to the store*, was mugged. (unnecessarily dividing the subject and verb)

CORRECT   *While walking to the store*, my neighbor was mugged.

Try this procedure in working with the following exercises.

1. Circle the modifier.
2. Draw an arrow from the modifier to the word or words it modifies.
3. If the modifier does not relate directly to anything in the sentence, it is dangling, and you must recast the sentence.
4. If the modifier does not modify the nearest word or words, or if it interrupts related sentence parts, it is misplaced and you need to reposition it.

Exercise 7 Correcting Dangling and Misplaced Modifiers

Circle the dangling (D) or misplaced (M) modifier in each of the following sentences. Identify the type of modifier by writing D or M in the blank to the left. Rewrite each sentence in the space provided.

_____ 1. Driving through the Brazilian rain forest, leaf-cutter ants were spotted going about their work.

_____ 2. This tribe of ants is one of the few creatures on this planet that grows food.

_____ 3. Leaf-cutter ants learned to cleverly farm more than 50 million years ago.

_____ 4. Climbing trees, the leaves are cut down and bitten into the shape of half-moons.

———   5. Then each ant hoists a leaf and carries it back down the tree toward the nest, weighing ten times more than it does.

_____

_____

———   6. Marching home with their leaves, a parade of fluttering green flags is what the ants resemble.

_____

_____

———   7. Carried into the subterranean tunnels of the nest, the leaf-cutters deposit their cargo.

_____

_____

———   8. Taking over, the leaves are cleaned, clipped, and spread with secretions from tiny gardener ants' bodies.

_____

_____

———   9. Lined up in neat rows, the ants place fungus on the hunks of leaves.

_____

_____

———   10. Cultivated for food, the ants use the leaves as fertilizer for their fungus garden.

_____

_____

Exercise 8   Correcting Dangling and Misplaced Modifiers

Circle the dangling (D) or misplaced (M) modifier in each of the following sentences. Identify the type of modifier by writing D or M in the blank to the left. Rewrite each sentence in the space provided.

_____ 1. I observed the parade of floats and marching bands on the rooftop.

_____

_____

_____ 2. Having no money, my piano had to be pawned for cash.

_____

_____

_____ 3. The alleged burglar addressed the judge on his knees.

_____

_____

_____ 4. Freshly snared from the ocean floor, he enjoyed the delicious lobster.

_____

_____

_____ 5. Wearing a strapless velvet evening gown, Bob thought his wife looked ravishing.

_____

_____

_____ 6. The student asked to see the school nurse with a sore throat.

_____

_____

_____ 7. The lost child held on tight to the detective crying for his mommy.

_____

_____

_____ 8. Cursing like a longshoreman, the baby finally arrived after her thirty-sixth hour of labor.

_____

_____

———— 9. By jumping on a trampoline, your heart gets a good
cardiovascular workout.

_____

_____

———— 10. The outlaw phoned his granny in a pickle.

_____

_____

⌒ Chapter Review

Exercise 9 Writing Sentences with Adjectives and Adverbs

Write a sentence using each of the following words.

1. good, better, best _____

_____

_____

_____

_____

_____

_____

2. good, well _____

_____

_____

_____

_____

_____

_____

3. more, most _____

_____

_____

_____

_____

_____

4. bad, badly _____

_____

_____

_____

_____

_____

5. real, really _____

_____

_____

_____

_____

_____

10

Punctuation and Capitalization

Understanding punctuation will help you write better. If you aren't sure how to punctuate a compound or a compound-complex sentence, then you probably will not write one. If you don't know how to show that some of your words come from other sources, you may mislead your reader. And if you misuse punctuation, you will force your readers to struggle to get your message. So take the time to review and master the mechanics. Your efforts will be rewarded.

∼ End Punctuation

Periods

1. Place a period after a statement.

    The weather is beautiful today.

2. Place a period after common abbreviations.

    Dr.   Mr.   Mrs.   Dec.   a.m.

    EXCEPTIONS: FBI   UN   NAACP   FHA   NATO

3. Use an ellipsis—three periods within a sentence and four periods at the end of a sentence—to indicate that words have been omitted from quoted material.

    He stopped walking and the buildings . . . rose up out of the misty courtroom. . . . (James Thurber, "The Secret Life of Walter Mitty")

152

Question Marks

1. Place a question mark at the end of a direct question.

   Will you go to the country tomorrow?

2. Use a single question mark in sentence constructions that contain a double question—that is, a quoted question within a question.

   Mr. Martin said, "Did he say, 'Are you going?'"

3. Do *not* use a question mark after an indirect (reported) question.

   She asked me what caused the slide.

Exclamation Points

1. Place an exclamation point after a word or a group of words that expresses strong feeling.

   Oh!   What a night!   Help!   You've got to be kidding!

2. Do not overwork the exclamation point. Do not use double exclamation points. Use the period or comma for mild exclamatory words, phrases, or sentences.

   Oh, we can leave now.

 Commas

Commas to Separate

1. Use a comma to separate main clauses joined by one of the coordinating conjunctions commonly referred to by the acronym FANBOYS: *for, and, nor, but, or, yet, so*. The comma may be omitted if the clauses are brief and parallel.

   We traveled many miles to see the game, *but* it was canceled.

   Adriana left and I remained. (brief and parallel clauses)

2. Use a comma after introductory dependent clauses and long introductory phrases (generally, four or more words is considered long).

   Before the arrival of the shipment, the boss had written a letter protesting the delay. (two prepositional phrases)

   If you don't hear from me, assume that I am lost. (introductory clause, an adverbial modifier)

   In winter we skate on the river. (short modifier, no comma)

3. Use a comma to separate words, phrases, and clauses in a series.

> *Red, white,* and *blue* were her favorite colors. (words)
>
> Ed drove *down the street, onto the freeway,* and *into the state of Texas.* (phrases)
>
> *When the television was off, when the children were in bed, and when the dog was asleep,* Mother could work on her research paper. (clauses)

4. Do *not* use a comma when coordinating conjunctions connect all the elements in a series.

> He bought apples *and* pears *and* grapes.

5. Use a comma to separate coordinate adjectives not joined by *and* that modify the same noun.

> I need a *sturdy, reliable* truck.

6. Use a comma to separate adjectives that are coordinate. Try this technique to determine whether the adjectives are coordinate: Put *and* between the adjectives. If it fits naturally, the adjectives are coordinate and require a comma; if it does not, they are not coordinate, and you do not need a comma.

> Wanda is a kind, beautiful person. (kind *and* beautiful—natural, hence the comma)
>
> I built a red brick wall. (red *and* brick wall—not natural, no comma)

7. Use a comma to separate sentence elements that might be misread.

> Inside the dog scratched his fleas.
>
> *Inside,* the dog scratched his fleas.

Without benefit of the comma, the reader might initially misunderstand the relationship among the first three words.

Commas to Set Off

1. Use commas to set off (enclose) adjectives in pairs that follow a noun.

> The scouts, *tired and hungry,* marched back to camp.

2. Use commas to set off nonessential (unnecessary for meaning of the sentence) words, phrases, and clauses.

My brother, *a student at Ohio University,* is visiting me. (If you drop the phrase, the basic meaning of the sentence remains intact.)

Marla, *who studied hard,* will pass. (The clause is not essential to the basic meaning of the sentence.)

All students *who studied hard* will pass. (Here the clause *is* essential. If you remove it, you would have *All students will pass,* which is not necessarily true.)

I shall not stop searching *until I find the treasure.* (A dependent clause at the end of a sentence is usually not set off with a comma. However, a clause beginning with the word *though, although,* or *whereas* will be set off regardless of where it is located.)

I felt unsatisfied, *though we had won the game.* (The clause begins with *though.*)

3. Use commas to set off parenthetical elements such as mild interjections (*oh, well, yes, no,* and others), most conjunctive adverbs (*however, otherwise, therefore, similarly, hence, on the other hand,* and *consequently,* but not *then, thus, soon, now,* and *also*), quotation indicators, and special abbreviations (*etc., i.e., e.g.,* and others).

Oh, what a silly question! (mild interjection)

It is necessary, *of course,* to leave now. (sentence modifier)

We left early; *however,* we missed the train anyway. (conjunctive adverb)

"When I was in school," *he said,* "I read widely." (quotation indicators)

Books, papers, pens, *etc.,* were scattered on the floor. (The abbreviation *etc.,* however, should be used sparingly.)

4. Use commas to set off nouns used as direct address.

Play it again, *Sam.*

Please tell us the answer, *Rashan,* so we can discuss it.

5. Use commas to separate the numbers in a date.

June *1, 1965,* is a day I will remember.

6. Do not use commas if the day of the month is not specified or if the day is given before the month.

June was my favorite time.

One day I will never forget is 4 June 1965.

7. Use commas to separate the city from the state. No comma is used between the state and the zip code.

    Walnut, CA 91789

8. Use a comma following the salutation of a friendly letter and the complimentary closing in any letter.

    Dear John,

    Sincerely,

9. Use a comma in numbers to set off groups of three digits. However, omit the comma in dates, serial numbers, page numbers, years, and street numbers.

    The total assets were $2,000,000.

    I look forward to the year 2012.

Exercise 1 Using Commas

Insert commas where needed.

1. In *Frankenstein* the original classic horror thriller written by

    Mary Shelley and published on October 3 1818 Victor

    Frankenstein was a gifted dedicated student.

2. While he studied science at the university he came upon the

    secret of how to create life.

3. Being more interested in simple practical matters than in

    theory he set out to construct a living breathing creature.

4. Victor who was very much concerned about process first

    needed to gather the materials necessary for his experiment.

5. He went all around town picking up body parts and he stored

    them in his laboratory.

6. The dissecting room at a local hospital provided him with the most basic articles and he was very grateful.

7. Local butcher shops had plenty of items perhaps including some spare ribs.

8. Finally he was ready to begin construction of a strange humanlike creature.

9. He made a creature that was eight feet tall four feet wide and very strong.

10. The face of the creature which could be described only as hideous was not easy to look upon.

11. One night while Victor was sleeping lightly the monster lonely and troubled came to his bedroom.

12. Victor screamed loudly and the monster ran away in disappointment.

13. Victor developed brain fever which was a result of the encounter.

14. When Victor recovered from his illness he discovered that one of his brothers had been murdered by an unknown person.

15. In despair and befuddlement Victor went to a remote wilderness to sort out his problems.

16. One day when he was out walking Victor saw a strange lumbering creature running into the mountains.

17. Victor chased the creature but he was unable to catch it.

18. Soon after he sat down to rest and the creature appeared

     before him.

19. It was Victor Frankenstein's monster who had come to talk

     to him.

20. With a great deal of self-pity the monster explained that he was

     very sad because people were unkind to him.

Exercise 2 Using Commas

Insert commas where needed.

1. Frankenstein's monster distraught and desperate told a story of

   acute loneliness.

2. After leaving Victor Frankenstein's house he had gone to live in

   the country.

3. He had tried diligently to help the simple gentle people by

   bringing them firewood.

4. They took the firewood; however they were at first frightened

   and then angry.

5. The monster very upset and dejected had gone back to the city.

6. There he killed Victor's innocent unsuspecting brother and he

   then cleverly tried to place the blame on someone else.

7. Listening to the monster in horror Victor Frankenstein realized what he had done in this act of creation.

8. The monster started making demands and it was clear that he would force Victor to carry them out.

9. He said that if Victor did not make a suitable female companion for him he would begin killing human beings at random.

10. Victor went away gathered up some more parts and started building a bride for the monster.

11. The monster waited in eager anticipation but he was to be sorely disappointed.

12. Victor became disgusted with his project and he destroyed all the tissue just before it came to life.

13. Needless to say the monster was deeply distressed by this unexpected shocking development.

14. Before the monster ran away he swore to get revenge on Victor's wedding night.

15. When Victor got married he armed himself fully for he expected a visit from the enraged vengeful monster.

16. On the night of the wedding the monster slipped into the bridal chambers and strangled the horrified unlucky bride.

17. Victor himself vowed to avenge the murder by killing the monster but the monster was nowhere to be found.

18. Victor finally died in a cabin in the desolate frozen lands of the North and much later his body was found by a friend.

19. The monster dropped by for one last visit for he wanted to complain about his unhappy life.

20. He said that Victor had created a man without a friend love or even a soul and therefore Victor was more wicked than anyone.

〜 Semicolons

The semicolon indicates a stronger division than the comma. It is used principally to separate independent clauses within a sentence.

1. Use a semicolon to separate independent clauses not joined by a coordinating conjunction.

    > You must buy that car today; tomorrow will be too late.

2. Use a semicolon between two independent clauses joined by a conjunctive adverb such as one of the HOTSHOT CAT words (*however, otherwise, therefore, similarly, hence, on the other hand, then, consequently, accordingly, thus*).

    > It was very late; therefore, I remained at the hotel.

3. Use a semicolon to separate main clauses joined by a coordinating conjunction if one or both of these clauses contain possibly distracting commas.

    > Byron, the famous English poet, was buried in Greece; and Shelley, who was his friend and fellow poet, was buried in Italy.

4. Use a semicolon in a series between items that themselves contain commas.

    > Lee has lived in Glendora, California; Fort Worth, Texas; Tribbey, Oklahoma; and Gulfport, Mississippi.

Exercise 3 Using Semicolons and Commas

Insert semicolons and commas where needed.

1. Once upon a time, there was a young woman named Cyberella she lived in Oklahoma with an evil stepmother and an obnoxious stepsister.

2. One night at eleven her wretched stepfamily was snoring raucously and Cyberella was busily dusting the family computer which someone had left running.

3. It was then that Cyberella inadvertently hit the Instant Internet button therefore the screen lit up.

4. She had never been permitted to use the Internet but she had enviously watched her evil stepfamily at the keyboard.

5. Cyberella created the screen name Cool4aday and logged on for fun and education naturally she started with the index of chat rooms.

6. She was delighted with her unexpected opportunity however she realized that the computer was programmed to go out of commission at midnight.

7. Now she was a free-spirited cyberspace explorer surfing the World Wide Web at midnight she would turn back into a servant ripping out cobwebs and capturing dust bunnies.

8. Cyberella spotted a chat room called "Talk to the Prince" feeling like a princess she joined in the conversation.

9. To her amazement she discovered that she was chatting with a real prince Prince Igor of Transylvania in fact he seemed to like her.

10. Prince Igor boldly invited Cyberella to accompany him to a private chat room breathlessly she said yes and followed him with demure keystrokes.

11. They chatted shyly and then passionately for almost an hour and soon the prince became royally enamored by the way she processed thought noticing that she wrote skillfully using her spell checker and grammar checker in a most delicate way.

12. Cyberella wanted to tell Prince Igor explicitly what was in her heart therefore she often used the computer thesaurus feature impressing him further with her highly eloquent diction.

13. Prince Igor was about to ask the royal marriage question then Cyberella heard the clock strike her computer went dark and she believed she would never again chat with her sweet prince.

14. Prince Igor was devastated and vowed to find this lovely correspondent he therefore directed his army to undertake a

royal search that would properly but legally identify Cool4aday and expose all impostors.

15. The soldiers would test the computer-assisted writing skills of everyone in the world if necessary moreover they would even provide laptops for any computerless woman who looked as if she could possibly be the mystery writer.

16. Cyberella had informed Prince Igor that she was from the American Southwest a fact that enabled him to focus his search.

17. Following electronic clues, the soldiers visited Amarillo Texas Tucumcari New Mexico Tulsa Oklahoma and Window Rock Arizona.

18. At last a soldier came to Cyberella's house and was greeted by the obnoxious stepsister who claimed that she was Cool4aday and began to chat online with Prince Igor however the stepsister forgot to use her spell checker and the prince flamed a rejection.

19. Then the soldier handed Cyberella a laptop computer and instructions of course both the wicked stepmother and the obnoxious stepsister scoffed.

20. Nevertheless, Cyberella was verified as Cool4aday and the prince was wildly elated therefore he declared an international holiday slapped his leg with glee and offered to grant her fondest wish.

21. "Does that mean I get this laptop for myself?" Cyberella asked

    and Prince Igor a bit humbled by her reponse said "No that

    means you get me for yourself."

22. "Oh, that's very very nice but may I also have this laptop?"

    Cyberella asked striking a hard bargain as she fondly hugged

    the computer.

23. "Yes" Prince Igor said. "I'll even toss in a laser printer and I'll

    add a few pounds of copy paper and a stack of dungeon-and-

    dragon software customized in one of my own castles."

24. They got married and lived happily ever after for a while then

    the wicked stepfamily tried to move into the palace but they

    were arrested and were no longer allowed to use the Internet in

    Transylvania or Oklahoma until they had passed a writing test

    which they never did.

〰 Quotation Marks

Quotation marks are used principally to set off direct quotations. A direct quotation consists of material taken from the written work or the direct speech of others; it is set off by double quotation marks. Single quotation marks are used to set off a quotation within a quotation.

DOUBLE QUOTATION MARKS	He said, "I don't remember."
SINGLE QUOTATION MARKS	He said, "I don't remember if she said, 'Wait for me.'"

1. Use double quotation marks to set off direct quotations.

> Jorell said, "Give me the book."
>
> As Edward McNeil writes of the Greek achievement: "To an extent never before realized, mind was supreme over faith."

2. Use double quotation marks to set off titles of shorter pieces of writing such as magazine articles, essays, short stories, short poems, one-act plays, chapters in books, songs, and separate pieces of writing published as part of a larger work.

> The book *Literature: Structure, Sound, and Sense* contains a deeply moving poem titled "On Wenlock Edge."
>
> Have you read "The Use of Force," a short story by William Carlos Williams?
>
> My favorite Elvis song is "Don't Be Cruel."

3. Use double quotation marks to set off slang, technical terms, and special words.

> There are many aristocrats, but Elvis is the only true "King." (special word)
>
> The "platoon system" changed the game of football. (technical term)

4. Use double quotation marks in writing dialogue (conversation). Write each speech unit as a separate paragraph and set it off with double quotation marks.

> "Will you go with me?" Cole asked.
>
> "Yes," Nikita replied. "Are you ready now?"

5. Use single quotation marks to set off a quotation within a quotation.

> Professor Baxter said, "You should remember Shakespeare's words 'All the world's a stage.'"

6. Do *not* use quotation marks for indirect quotations.

> WRONG   He said that "he would bring the supplies."
>
> RIGHT   He said that he would bring the supplies.

7. Do *not* use quotation marks for the title on your own written work. If you refer to that title in another piece of writing, however, you need the quotation marks.

〜 Punctuation with Quotation Marks

1. A period or comma is always placed *inside* the quotation marks.

   Our assignment for Monday was to read Poe's poem "The Raven."
   "I will read you the story," he said. "It's a good one."

2. A semicolon or colon is always placed *outside* the quotation marks.

   He read Robert Frost's poem "Design"; then he gave the examination.

3. A question mark, an exclamation point, or a dash is placed *outside* the quotation marks when it applies to the entire sentence and *inside* the quotation marks when it applies to the material in quotation marks.

   He asked, "Am I responsible for everything?" (quoted question within a statement)

   Did you hear him say, "I have the answer"? (statement within a question)

   Did she say, "Are you ready?" (question within a question)

   She shouted, "Impossible!" (exclamation)

   "I hope—that is, I—" he began. (dash)

〜 Italics

Italic print (slanting type) is used to call special attention to certain words or groups of words. In handwriting, such words are underlined.

1. Italicize (underline) foreign words and phrases that are still listed in the dictionary as foreign.

   c'est la vie   *Weltschmerz*

2. Italicize (underline) titles of books (except the Bible); long poems; plays; magazines; motion pictures; musical compositions; newspapers; works of art; names of aircraft; names of ships; and letters, figures, and words.

   I think Hemingway's best novel is *A Farewell to Arms.*

   His source material was taken from *Time, Newsweek,* and the Los Angeles *Times.* (Sometimes the name of the city in titles of newspapers is italicized—for example, the *New York Times*.)

The *Mona Lisa* is my favorite painting.

3. Italicize (underline) the names of ships, airplanes, spacecraft, and trains.

> *Queen Mary   Lurline   Stockholm*
> *Challenger   Voyager 2*

4. Italicize (underline) to distinguish letters, figures, and words when they refer to themselves rather than to the ideas or things they usually represent.

> Do not leave the *o* out of *sophomore*.
> Your *3*'s look like *5*'s.

Exercise 4 Using Quotation Marks and Italics

Insert quotation marks and italics (underlining) as needed.

1. Professor Jones said, Now we will read from The Complete Works of Edgar Allan Poe.

2. The enthusiastic students shouted, We like Poe! We like Poe!

3. The professor lectured for fifty-seven minutes before he finally said, In conclusion, Poe was an unappreciated writer during his lifetime.

4. The next speaker said, I believe that Poe said, A short story should be short enough so that a person can read it in one sitting.

5. Then, while students squirmed, he read The Fall of the House of Usher in sixty-eight minutes.

6. Now we will do some reading in unison, said Professor Jones.

7. The students were not pleased that they would be reading only the word *Nevermore* from the poem The Raven.

8. The professor reached into his bag of props, took out a dark, feathered object, and said, I have brought a stuffed raven.

9. That's not a raven. That's a crow, said a student who was majoring in ornithology.

10. The professor waggled his finger playfully at his audience and said, I believe Coleridge once observed, Art sometimes requires the willing suspension of disbelief.

Dashes

The dash is used when a stronger break than the comma is needed. The dash is typed as two hyphens with no space before or after them (--).

1. Use a dash to indicate a sudden change in sentence construction or an abrupt break in thought.

   Here is the true reason—but maybe you don't care.

2. Use a dash after an introductory list. The words *these, those, all,* and occasionally *such* introduce the summarizing statement.

   English, French, history—these are the subjects I like.

   Dodgers, Giants, Yankees—such names bring back memories of exciting World Series games.

3. Use a dash to set off material that interrupts the flow of an idea, sets off material for emphasis, or restates an idea as an appositive.

You are—I am certain—not serious. (interrupting)

Our next question is—how much money did we raise? (emphasis)

Dione plays the kazoo—an instrument with a buzz. (restatement)

4. Use a dash to indicate an unfinished statement, an omitted word, or an interruption. Such interruptions usually occur in dialogue.

Susan said, "Shall we—" (no period)

"I only wanted—" Jason remarked. (no comma)

5. Do *not* use a dash in places in which other marks of punctuation would be more appropriate.

WRONG   Lupe found the store—and she shopped.

RIGHT   Lupe found the store, and she shopped.

WRONG   I think it is too early to go—

RIGHT   I think it is too early to go.

∿ Colons

The colon is a formal mark of punctuation used chiefly to introduce something that is to follow, such as a list, a quotation, or an explanation.

1. Use a colon after a main clause to introduce a formal list, an emphatic or a long restatement (appositive), an explanation, an emphatic statement, or a summary.

These cars are my favorites: Cadillac, Chevrolet, Buick, Honda, and Toyota. (list)

He worked toward one objective: a degree. (restatement or appositive)

Let me emphasize one point: I do not accept late papers. (emphatic statement)

2. Use a colon to introduce a formal quotation or a formal question.

Shakespeare's Polonius said: "Neither a borrower nor a lender be." (formal quotation)

The question is this: Shall we surrender? (formal question)

3. Use a colon in the following conventional ways: to separate a title and subtitle, a chapter and verse in the Bible, and hours and minutes; and after the salutation in a formal business letter.

TITLE AND SUBTITLE *Korea: A Country Divided*
CHAPTER AND VERSE Genesis 4:12
HOUR AND MINUTES 8:25 p.m.
SALUTATION Dear Ms. Johnson:

∿ Parentheses

1. Parentheses are used to set off material that is not part of the main sentence but is too important to omit altogether. In this category are numbers that designate items in a series, amplifying references, explanations, directions, and qualifications.

> He offered two reasons for his losing: (1) he was tired; (2) he was out of condition. (numbers)
>
> Review the chapters on the Civil War (6, 7, and 8) for the next class meeting. (references)
>
> Her husband (she had been married about a year) died last week. (explanation)

2. Use a comma, semicolon, and colon after the parentheses when the sentence punctuation requires their use.

> Although I have not lived here long (I arrived in 2002), this place feels like my only true home.

Use a period, a question mark, and an exclamation point in appropriate positions, depending on whether they go with the material within the parentheses or with the entire sentence.

> The greatest English poet of the seventeenth century was John Milton (1608–1674).
>
> The greatest English poet of the seventeenth century was John Milton. (Some might not agree; I myself favor Andrew Marvell.)

∿ Brackets

Brackets are used within a quotation to set off editorial additions or corrections made by the person who is quoting.

> Churchill said: "It [the Yalta agreement] contained many mistakes."

⌒ Apostrophes

The apostrophe is used with nouns and indefinite pronouns to show possession; to show the omission of letters and figures in contractions; and to form the plurals of letters, figures, and words referred to as words.

1. A possessive shows that something is owned by someone. Use an apostrophe and -s to form the possessive of a noun, singular or plural, that does not end in -s.

   man's coat   women's suits

2. Use an apostrophe alone to form the possessive of a plural noun ending in -s.

   girls' clothes   the Browns' house

3. Use an apostrophe and -s or the apostrophe alone to form the possessive of singular nouns ending in -s. Use the apostrophe and -s only when you would pronounce the s.

   James' hat *or* (if you would pronounce the s) James's hat

4. Use an apostrophe and -s to form the possessive of certain indefinite pronouns.

   everybody's idea   one's meat   another's poison

5. Use an apostrophe to indicate that letters or figures have been omitted.

   o'clock (short for *of the clock*)   in the '80s (short for *1980s*)

6. Use an apostrophe to indicate the plural of letters, figures, and words used as words.

   Dot your *i*'s.   five 8's   *and*'s

7. Use an apostrophe with pronouns only when you are making a contraction. A contraction is a combination of two words. The apostrophe in a contraction indicates where a letter has been omitted.

   it is = it's
   she has = she's
   you are = you're

If no letters have been left out, don't use an apostrophe.

WRONG　The dog bit it's tail. (not a contraction)
RIGHT　The dog bit its tail.
WRONG　Whose the leader now?
RIGHT　Who's the leader now? (a contraction of *who is*)
WRONG　Its a big problem.
RIGHT　It's a big problem. (a contraction of *it is*)

∿ Hyphens

The hyphen brings two or more words together into a single compound word. Correct hyphenation, therefore, is essentially a spelling problem rather than one of punctuation. Because the hyphen is not used with any degree of consistency, consult your dictionary for current usage. Study the following as a beginning guide.

1. Use a hyphen to separate the parts of many compound words.

   brother-in-law　go-between

2. Use a hyphen between prefixes and suffixes and proper names.

   all-American　mid-Atlantic

3. Use a hyphen to join two or more words used as a single adjective modifier before a noun.

   bluish-gray eyes　first-class service

4. Use a hyphen with spelled-out compound numbers through ninety-nine, and with fractions.

   twenty-six　two-thirds

Note: Dates, street addresses, numbers requiring more than two words, chapter and page numbers, time followed directly by *a.m.* or *p.m.*, and figures after a dollar sign or before measurement abbreviations are usually written as figures, not words.

∿ Capitalization

In English, there are many conventions concerning the use of capital letters. Here are some of them.

1. Capitalize the first word of a sentence.
2. Capitalize proper nouns and adjectives derived from proper nouns.

> **Names of persons**
> Edward Jones
>
> **Adjectives derived from proper nouns**
> a Shakespearean sonnet   a Miltonic sonnet
>
> **Countries, nationalities, races, languages**
> Germany   English   Spanish   Chinese
>
> **States, regions, localities, other geographical divisions**
> California   the Far East   the South
>
> **Oceans, lakes, mountains, deserts, streets, parks**
> Lake Superior   Fifth Avenue   Sahara Desert
>
> **Educational institutions, schools, courses**
> Santa Ana College   Spanish 3   Joe Hill School
> Rowland High School
>
> **Organizations and their members**
> Boston Red Sox   Boy Scouts   Audubon Society
>
> **Corporations, governmental agencies or departments, trade names**
> U.S. Steel Corporation   Treasury Department
> White Memorial Library   Coke
>
> **Calendar references such as holidays, days of the week, months**
> Easter   Tuesday   January
>
> **Historic eras, periods, documents, laws**
> Declaration of Independence   Geneva Convention
> First Crusade   Romantic Age

3. Capitalize words denoting family relationships when they are used before a name or substituted for a name.

> Rex walked with his nephew and Aunt Grace.
> *but*
> Rex walked with his nephew and his aunt.
>
> Grandmother and Mother are away on vacation.
> *but*
> My grandmother and my mother are away on vacation.

4. Capitalize abbreviations after names.

> Henry White Jr.
> Juan Gomez, M.D.

5. Capitalize titles of themes, books, plays, movies, poems, magazines, newspapers, musical compositions, songs, and works of art. Do not capitalize short conjunctions and prepositions unless they come at the beginning or the end of the title.

> *Desire Under the Elms*   *Terminator*
>
> *Last of the Mohicans*   *Of Mice and Men*
>
> "Blueberry Hill"

6. Capitalize any title preceding a name or used as a substitute for a name. Do not capitalize a title following a name.

> Judge Wong   Alfred Wong, a judge
>
> General Clark   Raymond Clark, a general
>
> Professor Fuentes   Harry Jones, the former president

Exercise 5   Using Capital Letters and All Punctuation Marks

Correct capitalization and insert punctuation marks as needed.

will rogers 1879–1935 was a famous movie star newspaper writer and lecturer. A part cherokee indian he was born in what was then indian territory before oklahoma became a state. He is especially known for his humor and his social and political criticism. He said my ancestors may not have come over on the *mayflower,* but they met em at the boat. He said that when many oklahomans moved to california in the early1930s the average IQ increased in both states. In his early years, he was a first class performer in rodeos circuses and variety shows. When he performed in variety shows he often twirled a rope. He usually began his presentations by saying all I know is what I read in the papers. Continuing to be close to his oklahoma roots he appeared in fifty one silent movies and twenty one talking movies. At the age of fifty six he was killed in an airplane crash near Point Barrow Alaska. He was so popular and influential that his statue now stands in washington d.c. On another statue of him in Claremore Oklahoma is inscribed one of his most famous sayings I never met a man I didn't like.

Exercise 6 Using Capital Letters and All Punctuation Marks

Correct capitalization and insert punctuation marks as needed.

Jack (Jackie) Roosevelt Robinson 1919–1972 was born in Pasadena California. After excelling in sports in high school and community college he transferred to UCLA, where he lettered in four sports baseball, basketball, football, and track. In world war II he was commissioned second lieutenant in the army. After he was discharged he joined the negro league as a player with the Kansas City Monarchs for $100 a week. In 1947 he was offered a tryout with the Brooklyn dodgers. Before no African Americans had been allowed to participate in the minor or major leagues. After signing a contract, Jackie Robinson was sent to the minor leagues and there he played for one year with Montreal a team in the International League. Following a year in which he was the best hitter in the league he was brought up to the major leagues. During the first year 1947 he showed his greatness and was named the rookie of the year. Two years later he was the most valuable player in the national league and won the batting title with a .342 average. Despite the initial bigoted opposition by some baseball fans and players he performed with dignity courage and skill. Nevertheless he was an independent proud person. In the book Players of Cooperstown Mike Tully wrote he Robinson refused to be someone he was not, refused to conform to an image of a man who 'knew his place.' Because sports is such a high profile activity Jackie Robinson is credited with playing a significant role in breaking down the racial barriers in society. In his ten years in the major leagues he helped his team reach the world series six times. He was inducted into the Baseball hall of fame in 1962.

⌒ Chapter Review

Exercise 7 Writing Sentences with Correct Punctuation

Demonstrate your ability to use punctuation by writing sentences that contain these marks. Use the topics in parentheses.

Comma (travel)

1. To separate independent clauses in a compound sentence using a coordinating conjunction, FANBOYS (*for, and, nor, but, or, yet, so*) _____

   _____

   _____

2. For long introductory modifiers (*because, after, that, when, as, since, how, till, unless, before,* and others) _____

_____

_____

3. To separate words in a series _____

_____

Semicolon (a family member)

4. To connect two related independent clauses without a coordinating conjunction _____

_____

_____

Quotation Marks (Use this textbook as your source for quotations.)

5. To set off a quotation (words taken from the written work or the speech of others) _____

_____

_____

Italics, shown by underlining (school)

6. To refer to a word or letter by its name _____

_____

_____

7. For the title of a book _____

_____

_____

Colon (a job)

8. To introduce a list _____

_____

_____

Apostrophe (friendship)

9. To show a singular or plural possessive _____

_____

_____

10. To write a contraction _____

_____

_____

Hyphen (shopping)

11. To use in numbers _____

_____

_____

12. To indicate two-word modifiers _____

_____

_____

11

Spelling and Commonly Confused Words

Spelling Tips

The following tips will help you become a better speller:

- **Do not omit letters.**

  Many errors occur because certain letters are omitted when the word is pronounced or spelled. Observe the omissions in the following words. Then concentrate on learning the correct spellings.

Incorrect	Correct	Incorrect	Correct
agravate	aggravate	ajourned	adjourned
aproved	approved	aquaintance	acquaintance
artic	arctic	comodity	commodity
efficent	efficient	envirnment	environment
familar	familiar	irigation	irrigation
libary	library	paralell	parallel
parlament	parliament	paticulaly	particularly
readly	readily	sophmore	sophomore
stricly	strictly	unconsious	unconscious

- **Do not add letters.**

Incorrect	Correct	Incorrect	Correct
athelete	athlete	comming	coming
drownded	drowned	folkes	folks
occassionally	occasionally	ommission	omission
pasttime	pastime	priviledge	privilege
similiar	similar	tradgedy	tragedy

179

- **Do not substitute incorrect letters for correct letters.**

Incorrect	Correct	Incorrect	Correct
benefisial	beneficial	bullitins	bulletins
sensus	census	discription	description
desease	disease	dissention	dissension
itims	items	offence	offense
peculier	peculiar	resitation	recitation
screach	screech	substansial	substantial
surprize	surprise	technacal	technical

- **Do not transpose letters.**

Incorrect	Correct	Incorrect	Correct
alunmi	alumni	childern	children
dupilcate	duplicate	irrevelant	irrelevant
kindel	kindle	prehaps	perhaps
perfer	prefer	perscription	prescription
principels	principles	yeild	yield

Note: Whenever you notice other words that fall into any one of these categories, add them to the list.

- **Apply the spelling rules for spelling *ei* and *ie* words correctly.**

  Remember the poem?

  Use *i* before *e*
  Except after *c*
  Or when sounded as *a*
  As in *neighbor* and *weigh*.

  i before e

achieve	belief	believe	brief
chief	field	grief	hygiene
niece	piece	pierce	relief
relieve	shield	siege	variety

  Except after c

ceiling	conceit	conceive	deceit
deceive	perceive	receipt	receive

  Exceptions: either, financier, height, leisure, neither, seize, species, weird.

*When sounded as **a***

deign	eight	feign	feint
freight	heinous	heir	neigh
neighbor	rein	reign	skein
sleigh	veil	vein	weigh

- **Apply the rules for dropping the final *e* or retaining the final *e* when a suffix is added.**

Words ending in a silent *e* usually drop the *e* before a suffix beginning with a vowel; for example, *accuse + -ing = accusing*. Some common suffixes beginning with a vowel are the following: *-able, -al, -age, -ary, -ation, -ence, -ing, -ion, -ous, -ure*.

admire + *-able* = admirable   arrive + *-al* = arrival
come + *-ing* = coming   explore + *-ation* = exploration
fame + *-ous* = famous   imagine + *-ary* = imaginary
locate + *-ion* = location   please + *ure* = pleasure
plume + *-age* = plumage   precede + *-ence* = precedence

Exceptions: dye + -ing = dyeing (to distinguish it from *dying*), *acreage, mileage.*

Words ending in a silent *e* usually retain the *e* before a suffix beginning with a consonant; for example: *arrange + -ment = arrangement*. Some common suffixes beginning with a consonant are the following: *-craft, -ful, -less, -ly, -mate, -ment, -ness, -ty*.

entire + *-ty* = entirety   hate + *-ful* = hateful
hope + *-less* = hopeless   like + *-ness* = likeness
manage + *-ment* = management   safe + *-ly* = safely
stale + *-mate* = stalemate   state + *-craft* = statecraft

Exceptions: Some words taking the *-ful* or *-ly* suffixes drop the final *e*:

awe + *-ful* = awful   due + *-ly* = duly
true + *-ly* = truly   whole + *-ly* = wholly

Some words taking the suffix *-ment* drop the final *e*; for example:

acknowledgment   argument   judgment

Words ending in silent *e* after *c* or *g* retain the *e* when the suffix begins with the vowel *a* or *o*. The final *e* is retained to keep the *c* or *g* soft before the suffixes.

advantageous   courageous
noticeable   peaceable

- **Apply the rules for doubling a final consonant before a suffix beginning with a vowel.**

Words of one syllable

blot	blotted	brag	bragging	cut	cutting
drag	dragged	drop	dropped	get	getting
hop	hopper	hot	hottest	man	mannish
plan	planned	rob	robbed	run	running
sit	sitting	stop	stopped	swim	swimming

Words accented on the last syllable

acquit	acquitted	admit	admittance
allot	allotted	begin	beginning
commit	committee	concur	concurring
confer	conferring	defer	deferring
equip	equipped	occur	occurrence
omit	omitting	prefer	preferred
refer	referred	submit	submitted
transfer	transferred		

Words that are not accented on the last syllable or words that do not end in a single consonant preceded by a vowel do not double the final consonant (regardless of whether the suffix begins with a vowel).

～ Frequently Misspelled Words

a lot	beginning	dependent	environment
absence	belief	develop	especially
across	benefit	development	etc.
actually	buried	difference	exaggerate
all right	business	disastrous	excellent
among	certain	discipline	exercise
analyze	college	discussed	existence
appearance	coming	disease	experience
appreciate	committee	divide	explanation
argument	competition	dying	extremely
athlete	complete	eighth	familiar
athletics	consider	eligible	February
awkward	criticism	eliminate	finally
becoming	definitely	embarrassed	foreign

government	meant	pursue	speech
grammar	medicine	receipt	straight
grateful	neither	receive	studying
guarantee	ninety	recommend	succeed
guard	ninth	reference	success
guidance	nuclear	relieve	suggest
height	occasionally	religious	surprise
hoping	opinion	repetition	thoroughly
humorous	opportunity	rhythm	though
immediately	parallel	ridiculous	tragedy
independent	particular	sacrifice	tried
intelligence	persuade	safety	tries
interest	physically	scene	truly
interfere	planned	schedule	unfortunately
involved	pleasant	secretary	unnecessary
knowledge	possible	senior	until
laboratory	practical	sense	unusual
leisure	preferred	separate	using
length	prejudice	severely	usually
library	privilege	shining	Wednesday
likely	probably	significant	writing
lying	professor	similar	written
marriage	prove	sincerely	
mathematics	psychology	sophomore	

Exercise 1 Using Correct Spelling

Underline the misspelled words and write the correct spelling above the words. Double underline the words that are incorrectly spelled but would go unchallenged by your spell checker.

Professor Pufnagel was torturing his English students once again, and he relished his familar evil roll. "Today, class, we will write without the assistence of computers. In fact, never again will we use them in this class. They are a perscription for lazyness. And they make life to easy for alot of you."

The profesor lectured the students for an hour, stresing that when he was in school, there were no computers in his enviroment. He extoled the virtues of writting with little yellow pensils, fountain pens, and solid, dependible typewriters. He went on with his ranting, listing computer games, television sets, frozen foods, plastic wrap, asperin, and Velcro as similiar and familiar negative forces that had lead society to it's truely sorry state. "You are nothing but a pityful pack of party people, and you will recieve no sympathy from me," he sputtered. Grabbing a student's laptop computer, Pufnagel reared back and, like an athalete, hurled it against the wall. In the corner of the classroom lay a pile of high-tech junk, once fine shinning machines, now just garbage—smashed in a senseless, aweful war against technology.

The students starred in embarassed amazement at there professor, who was developing a nervous twitch. His mouth began twisting and contorting as his limbs jerked with the helter-skelter motion of a tangled marionette. He clutched desparately at his throat, and smoke began to poor out of his ears and neck. Unconsious, he crashed to the floor with a clatter.

One of the students, who had just taken a CPR class, rushed forward and attempted to revive the fallen educator. As the student pounded with a catchy rap rhythem on the chest of his stricken teacher, everyone herd a loud pop and sizzle.

It was a door in Pufnagel's chest, which had poped open to reveal the complex electrical control panel of a short-circuited cyborg!

Just than a security team in white jumpsuits from student goverment entered the class, carefully deposited Pufnagel on a wheelbarrow, and roled him out to the Faculty Service Center.

A few minutes later a Professor Ramirez arrived. "Ladys and gentlemen," she said, "its time to start your search engines. Your prevous professor's mainframc is down, but I'm his substitute and mine is finc, fine, fine, fine, fine, fine, fine, fine, fine, fine. . . ."

◯ Confused Spelling / Confusing Words

The following arc more words that arc commonly misspelled or confused with one another. Some have similar sounds, some are often mispronounced, and some are only misunderstood.

a	An article adjective used before a word beginning with a consonant or a consonant sound, as in "I ate *a* donut."
an	An article adjective used before a word beginning with a vowel (*a, e, i, o, u*) or with a silent *h*, as in "I ate *an* artichoke."
and	A coordinating conjunction, as in "Sara *and* I like Johnny Cash."
accept	A verb meaning "to receive," as in "I *accept* your explanation."

except	A preposition meaning "to exclude," as in "I paid everyone *except* you."
advice	A noun meaning "guidance," as in "Thanks for the *advice*."
advise	A verb meaning "to give guidance," as in "Will you please *advise* me of my rights?"
all right	An adjective meaning "correct" or "acceptable," as in "It's *all right* to cry."
alright	Not used in formal writing.
all ready	An adjective that can be used interchangeably with *ready*, as in "I am *all ready* to go to town."
already	An adverb meaning "before," which cannot be used in place of *ready*, as in "I have *already* finished."
a lot	An adverb meaning "much," as in "She liked him *a lot*," or a noun meaning "several," as in "I had *a lot* of suggestions."
alot	Misspelling.
altogether	An adverb meaning "completely," as in "He is *altogether* happy."
all together	An adverb meaning "as one," which can be used interchangeably with *together*, as in "The group left *all together*."
could of	Misspelling.
could have	A verb phrase, as in "I *could have* used some kindness."
choose	A present tense verb meaning "to select," as in "Do whatever you *choose*."
chose	The past tense form of the verb *choose*, as in "They *chose* to take action yesterday."
effect	Usually a noun meaning "result," as in "That *effect* was unexpected."
affect	Usually a verb meaning "change," as in "Ideas *affect* me."
hear	A verb indicating the receiving of sound, as in "I *hear* thunder."
here	An adverb meaning "present location," as in "I live *here*."
it's	A contraction of *it is*, as in "*It's* time to dance."
its	Possessive pronoun, as in "Each dog has *its* day."

know	A verb usually meaning "to comprehend" or "to recognize," as in "I *know* the answer."
no	An adjective meaning "negative," as in "I have *no* potatoes."
led	The past tense form of the verb *lead*, as in "I *led* a wild life in my youth."
lead	A present tense verb, as in "I *lead* a stable life now" or a noun referring to a substance, such as "I sharpened the *lead* in my pencil."
loose	An adjective meaning "without restraint," as in "He is a *loose* cannon."
lose	A present tense verb from the pattern *lose, lost, lost*, as in "I thought I would *lose* my senses."
paid	The past tense form of *pay*, as in "He *paid* his dues."
payed	Misspelling.
passed	The past tense form of the verb *pass*, meaning "went by," as in "He *passed* me on the curve."
past	An adjective meaning "former," as in "That's *past* history"; or a noun, as in "the past."
patience	A noun meaning "willingness to wait," as in "Job was a man of much *patience*."
patients	A noun meaning "people under care," as in "The doctor had fifty *patients*."
peace	A noun meaning "a quality of calmness" or "absence of strife," as in "The guru was at *peace* with the world."
piece	A noun meaning "part," as in "I gave him a *piece* of my mind."
quiet	An adjective meaning "silent," as in "She was a *quiet* child."
quit	A verb meaning "to cease" or "to withdraw," as in "I *quit* my job."
quite	An adverb meaning "very," as in "The clam is *quite* happy."
receive	A verb meaning "to accept," as in "I will *receive* visitors now."
recieve	Misspelling.
stationary	An adjective meaning "not moving," as in "Try to avoid running into *stationary* objects."

stationery	A noun meaning "paper material to write on," as in "I bought a box of *stationery* for Sue's birthday present."
than	A conjunction, as in "He is taller *than* I am."
then	An adverb, as in "She *then* left town."
their	An adjective, as in "They read *their* books."
there	An adverb, as in "He left it *there*," or a filler word as in "*There* is no time left."
they're	A contraction of *they are*, as in "*They're* happy."
to	A preposition, as in "I went *to* town."
too	An adverb meaning "having exceeded or gone beyond what is acceptable," as in "You are *too* late to qualify for the discount," or "also," as in "I have feelings, *too*."
two	An adjective of number, as in "I have *two* jobs."
thorough	An adjective, as in "He did a *thorough* job."
through	A preposition, as in "She went *through* the yard."
truly	An adverb meaning "sincerely" or "completely," as in "He was *truly* happy."
truely	Misspelling.
weather	A noun meaning "condition of the atmosphere," as in "The *weather* is pleasant today."
whether	A conjunction, as in "*Whether* he would go was of no consequence."
write	A present tense verb, as in "Watch me as I *write* this letter."
writen	Misspelling.
written	A past participle verb, as in "I have *written* the letter."
you're	A contraction of *you are*, as in "*You're* my friend."
your	A possessive pronoun, as in "I like *your* looks."

Exercise 2   Spelling Confusing Words

Underline the correct word or words.

1. I cannot (hear, here) the answers.

2. Isabella is taller (then, than) I.

3. They left town to find (their, they're, there) roots.

4. Sam went (through, thorough) the initiation.

5. I am only asking for a little (peace, piece) of the action.

6. Whatever you say is (alright, all right) with me.

7. I (passed, past) the test, and now I'm ready for action.

8. That smash was (to, too, two) hot to handle.

9. I did not ask for her (advise, advice).

10. I found (a lot, alot) of new ideas in that book.

11. Marilyn has (all ready, already) left.

12. I (chose, choose) my answer and hoped for the best.

13. I knew that I would (recieve, receive) fair treatment.

14. Juan was (quit, quite, quiet) happy with my decision.

15. Maria (could of, could have) completed the assignment.

16. Marlin knew they would (lose, loose) the game.

17. I've heard that (it's, its) a good movie.

18. June would not (accept, except) my answer.

19. I did not (know, no) what to do.

20. Sean (paid, payed) his bill and left town.

Exercise 3 Spelling Confusing Words

Underline the correct word or words.

1. Erin said that my application was (alright, all right).

2. Sheriff Andy Griffin worked hard for (peace, piece) in Mayberry.

3. Lauren was the first woman to (recieve, receive) a medal.

4. Shane spoke his mind; (then, than) he left.

5. The cleaners did a (through, thorough) job.

6. After the loud explosion, there was (quit, quiet, quite).

7. The nurse worked diligently with his (patience, patients).

8. They were not (altogether, all together) happy, but they (could of, could have) been.

9. The cowboys (led, lead) the cows to water.

10. For my hobby, I study (grammar, grammer).

11. Elvis (truly, truely) respected his mother.

12. Jarrett asked for the (whether, weather) report.

13. I never (advise, advice) my friends about gambling.

14. You should (accept, except) responsibility for your actions.

15. Matthew inherited (alot, a lot) of money.

16. We waited for the gorilla to (chose, choose) a mate.

17. Virginia thinks (its, it's) a good day for a party.

18. It was a tale of (to, too, two) cities.

19. I went (they're, their, there) to my childhood home.

20. It was the best letter Kevin had ever (writen, written, wrote).

〜 Wordy Phrases

Certain phrases clutter sentences, consuming our time in writing and our readers' time in reading. Watch for wordy phrases as you revise and edit your composition.

WORDY   *Due to the fact* that he was unemployed, he had to use public transportation.

CONCISE   *Because* he was unemployed, he had to use public transportation.

WORDY   *Deep down inside* he believed that the Red Sox would win.

CONCISE   He believed that the Red Sox would win.

Wordy	Concise
at the present time	now
basic essentials	essentials
blend together	blend
it is clear that	(delete)
due to the fact that	because
for the reason that	because
I felt inside	I felt
in most cases	usually
as a matter of fact	in fact
in the event that	if
until such time as	until
I personally feel	I feel
in this modern world	today
in order to	to
most of the people	most people
along the lines of	like
past experience	experience
at that point in time	then
in the final analysis	finally
in the near future	soon
have a need for	need
in this day and age	now

Exercise 4 Avoiding Wordy Phrasing

Circle the wordy phrases and write in concise phrases.

1. I tried to recall that moment, but my memories seemed to blend together.

2. I expect to get out of this bed and go to work in the near future.

3. As a matter of fact, when I was a child, I had an imaginary playmate.

4. I feel in my heart that bees work too hard.

5. I am not surprised by his conviction due to the fact that as a child he used to torment vegetables.

6. In this modern world most of the people do not use enough shoe polish.

7. I was crowned Mr. Clean for the reason that I always wash my hands before I wash my hands.

8. At the present time I am concentrating on not thinking about warthogs.

9. Procrastination is an idea I will consider in the near future.

10. I personally feel that Cupid just shot me with a poisoned arrow.

12

The Writing Process: Paragraphs and Essays

∿ The Paragraph and Essay Defined

A **paragraph** is a group of sentences that relate to a single idea. That idea, called the **controlling idea**, is often stated in one sentence, which is known as the topic sentence. All the other sentences in the paragraph explain or support the topic sentence.

An **essay** contains multiple paragraphs. It begins with an introductory paragraph that usually presents the main idea (or thesis). The main idea is then developed in several paragraphs that make up the body of the essay. An essay usually ends with a concluding paragraph that gives a feeling of finality, or closure. The concluding paragraph sometimes summarizes the main idea that was developed throughout the essay.

Thus, considered structurally, the paragraph is often an essay in miniature. That does not mean that all paragraphs can grow up to be essays or that all essays can shrink to become paragraphs. For college writing, however, a good understanding of the parallel between well-organized paragraphs and well-organized essays is useful. As you learn the properties of effective paragraphs—those with a strong topic sentence and strong support—you also learn how to organize an essay, if you just magnify the procedure.

The following diagram illustrates the parallel parts of many outlines, paragraphs, and essays:

PARAGRAPH	OUTLINE	ESSAY
Topic Sentence	Topic Sentence or Thesis	Introduction, with Thesis or Purpose
Support Sentence 1	I. Support 1	Support Paragraph 1
Support Sentence 2	II. Support 2	Support Paragraph 2
Support Sentence 3	III. Support 3	Support Paragraph 3
Concluding Sentence	Conclusion	Conclusion

193

〰 The Writing Process

Effective and easily followed steps exist for writing a paragraph and even an essay. Writing does not mean merely putting words on a piece of paper. It is a process that often involves several stages: using prewriting techniques to explore a topic; limiting and then developing the topic, usually with an outline; writing a first draft; revising the draft as often as necessary; and editing the material. At times, writers discover that their topic sentence or their outline does not work, and they go back and alter their original concept or design.

Here is how one student, Vera Harris, moved from an idea to a topic sentence to an outline to a paragraph. Vera Harris returned to college while she still had a full-time job as a hairdresser. When her instructor asked her to write a paragraph about types of people she had encountered, she naturally considered her customers for the subject of her paragraph—what she would write about. But she also had a special interest in dogs, and she hoped she would be able, somehow, to include that interest. Although she knew her topic rather well, she worked with some prewriting techniques that allowed her to get her ideas flowing onto paper.

Prewriting

Freewriting

Vera wrote about a page without stopping, just letting her ideas tumble forward without concern for correctness. This enabled her to get her project under way and to deal immediately with the common problem of writer's block. She knew that most of the material would be unusable but also that she would probably hit on some good ideas that would give her a sense of direction and new insights. These good ideas she would circle and perhaps even make notes about in the margins of her paper. Here is Vera's freewriting.

```
    I have worked in beauty shops for a long time and
I've naturally made a lot of observations about my
customers. I could write about what they look like and
how they behave and how they tip and lots of things. When
```

I first started to work I guess at first I thought of them as pretty much the same but then I started to see them as types mainly as to how they acted and I remember way back then I sometimes thought of how they reminded me of dogs. I don't mean that in any bad way but just that human beings have their personalities and their appearances and all and so do dogs.

Brainstorming

Vera then sharpened her focus by listing some words and phrases, mainly in response to the questions *Who? What? Where? When? Why?* and *How?* One (*How?*) became a list.

Who? my customers
What? the way they act
Where? in the beauty salon
When? for the years I have worked
Why? their basic nature
How? behavior sometimes like dogs—hounds, Dobermans, terriers, bulldogs, cockers, poodles, mixed, retrievers, boxers

Clustering

After indicating her main subject inside a double bubble, Vera jotted down ideas inside single bubbles radiating out from the topic hub, as shown in the cluster on page 196. With this arrangement, she could begin to see connections.

Topic Sentence

At that point, knowing her subject material and the assignment very well, Vera wrote a topic sentence. A **topic sentence** controls the paragraph by indicating the subject (what the writer is writing about) and the focus (what the writer is doing with the subject) of the subject.

The customers in the beauty shop where I work
subject

remind me of types of dogs (of which I am fond).
focus

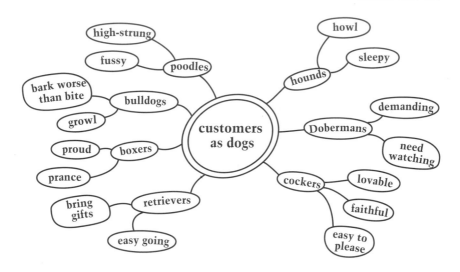

Outline

Then Vera made a basic outline. An **outline** is a pattern for showing the relationship of ideas. Vera supported her topic sentence by listing the types of dogs her customers reminded her of. Under each type, she described the characteristics typical of both the dogs and the people. The major-support and minor-support labels show you how she organized her material in correct outline form.

> TOPIC SENTENCE   The customers in the beauty shop where I work remind me of types of dogs (of which I am fond).

I. Poodles (major support)
   A. High-strung (minor support)
   B. Need attention (minor support)
II. Doberman pinschers (major support)
   A. Demanding (minor support)
   B. Need watching (minor support)
III. Bulldogs (major support)
   A. Act mean (minor support)
   B. Will back down (minor support)
IV. Cocker spaniels (major support)
   A. Lovable (minor support)
   B. Faithful (minor support)
   C. Easy to please (minor support)

If Vera had experienced problems, she would have gone back to her topic sentence or even to her prewriting to make adjustments.

Writing a First Draft

Following her outline for her main and supporting points, Vera wrote her first draft. (With more development, this writing could have been a six-paragraph essay instead of a long paragraph. See the diagram on page 193.) In a first draft, writers do not try to "get everything right." They try to discuss the topic as fully as possible. Here is Vera's first draft:

```
            Customers Are Like Canines

    I have worked in a beauty salon for a long time.

There, I have come across almost every kind of salon

customer, each with her own unique looks and personality.

I am also a dog lover and I have observed numerous dogs

with care it is easier to classify these people if I

compare them with canine types—but in a playful rather

than a mean way. The first group is made up of poodles.

Poodles are very prissy, with a constant need for

attention. Their hair is usually over-styled. They think

puffballs in soft colors look great. The next group and

largest group is made up of cocker spaniels. The cockers

are very lovable the most faithful. They like being

pampered. Cockers like to see me every week and visit

with others. Sometimes I can almost see their tails

wagging. Then come the Doberman pinchers, this type

scares me the most. Dobies are hard to please. If one

hair goes the wrong way. I will see their upper lip rise

up to show eyeteeth, as if they are snarling. I rarely

turn my back while working on this type—a Dobie might
```

```
bite. The last group the bulldogs, are not as mean as

Dobies Bulldogs act mean and tough, but if you don't show

fear when they get bossy they will back down. This type

needs to feel in charge, even if it's me leading them

around on a leash.
```

Revising and Editing

After writing her first draft, Vera began revising her paragraph. To revise is to rearrange and polish the writing, putting the sentences in the best possible order and coming up with the best possible words. Vera used the acronym CLUESS to remember her revision checklist.

Coherence: Does the material flow smoothly from each idea, leading logically and evenly to the next?

Language: Are the words appropriate for the message, occasion, and audience (avoiding slang, clichés, and worn-out expressions)?

Unity: Are all the ideas related and subordinate to the topic sentence?

Emphasis: Are techniques such as repetition and careful placement of words and ideas used to emphasize the main points?

Support: Do details, examples, and similar material back up, justify, or prove the topic sentence?

Sentences: Is there some variety in sentence structure? Have fragments, comma splices, and run-ons been corrected?

Finally, Vera edited her paper. To edit is to correct the basic writing errors that have been overlooked. Vera used the acronym COPS to remember the one question that would cover her concerns: Are there problems with **c**apitalization, **o**missions, **p**unctuation, and spelling?

Here is Vera's first draft, revised and edited.

Customers Are Like Canines

language
punctuation

Over the years while working
~~I have worked~~ in a beauty salon~~, for a~~

~~long time. There,~~ I have come across almost

every kind of salon customer, each with her

Because

sentences   own unique looks and personality. I am also a

dog lover and ~~I~~ have observed numerous dogs

punctuation   with care, it is easier to classify these

relate them to

language   people if I compare ~~them with~~ canine types—

logic   but in a playful rather than a mean way. The

first group is made up of poodles. Poodles

and high-strung

language   are very prissy, with a constant need for

attention. Their hair is usually over styled.

They think puffballs in soft colors look

last

great. The ~~next~~ group and largest group is

emphasis
spelling   made up of cocker spaniels. The Cockers are
omission

and   *enjoy*

very lovable, the most faithful. They ~~like~~

groomed and stroked, but they are easy to please.

language   being ~~pampered~~. Cockers like to see me every

to

week and visit with others. Sometimes I can

almost see their tails wagging. Then come the

s   *T*

sentences   Doberman pinchers. this type scares me the

most. Dobies are hard to please. If one hair

sentences   goes the wrong way⸮ I will see their upper lip

       expose
language   rise up to ~~show~~ eyeteeth⊙ ~~as if they are~~

~~snarling.~~ I rarely turn my back while working

                third—
punctuation   on this type—a Dobie might bite. The ~~last~~

    members,
group the bulldogs, are not as mean as Dobies⊙

               one doesn't
language   Bulldogs act mean and tough, but if ~~you don't~~

punctuation   show fear when they get bossy they will back

down. This type needs to feel in charge, even

    I'm
language   if ~~it's me~~ leading them around on a leash.
No matter what, canines and customers are my best friends.

Here is Vera's final draft:

Customers Are Like Canines

topic   Over the years while working in a beauty
sentence

salon, I have come across almost every kind

of salon customer, each with her own unique

looks and personality. Because I am also a dog

lover and have observed numerous dogs with

care, it is easier to classify these people if

support   I relate them to canine types—but in a playful

rather than a mean way. The first group is made

up of poodles. Poodles are very prissy and

high-strung, with a constant need for

attention. Their hair is usually overstyled.

They think puffballs in soft colors look great.

support   Then come the Doberman pinschers. This type

scares me the most. Dobies are hard to please.

If one hair goes the wrong way, I will see

their upper lip rise up to expose eyeteeth. I

rarely turn my back while working on this type—

support   a Dobie might bite. The third-group members,

the bulldogs, are not as mean as Dobies.

Bulldogs act mean and tough, but if one doesn't

show fear when they get bossy, they will back

down. This type needs to feel in charge, even

support   if I'm leading them around on a leash. The

last—and largest—group is made up of cocker

spaniels. The cockers are very lovable and the

most faithful. They enjoy being groomed and

stroked, but they are easy to please. Cockers

like to see me every week and to visit with

others. Sometimes I can almost see their tails

wagging. No matter what, canines and customers

are my best friends.

∿ The Writing Process Worksheet

The Writing Process Worksheet on page 202 (and also on the Student Companion Site) may help you move from assignment to the final paragraph or essay. Your instructor may ask you to enlarge the page on a photocopier, complete it, and submit it with your final paper. It can direct you through the stages of writing and show your instructor how you proceeded.

Writing Process Worksheet

Title _____

Name _____ Due Date _____

Use separate paper if you need more space.

Assignment   In the space below, write whatever you need to know
about your assignment, including information about
the topic, audience, pattern of writing, length, whether
to include a rough draft or revised drafts, and whether
your paper must be typed.

Stage One   **Explore**   Freewrite, brainstorm (list), cluster, or take
notes as directed by your instructor.

Stage Two   **Organize**   Write a topic sentence or thesis; label the
subject and focus parts.

Write an outline or a structured list. For reading-based
writing, include references and short quotations with
page numbers within the outline.

Stage Three   **Write**   On separate paper, write and then revise your
paragraph or essay as many times as necessary for **co-**
herence, language (usage, tone, and diction), **u**nity, **e**m-
phasis, support, and sentences (**CLUESS**). Read your
work aloud to hear and correct any grammatical errors
or awkward-sounding sentences.

Edit any problems in fundamentals, such as **c**apitalization, **o**missions, **p**unctuation, and spelling (**COPS**).

13

Combined and Specific Patterns of Writing and Writing Topics

∼ Combined Patterns of Writing

Organization in a sound paragraph or essay reflects the intention of the author in fulfilling the needs of a writing task. As that writer, you begin by asking yourself what you are trying to say and who your audience is. If you are attempting to compare and contrast subject material, such as generations or leaders, then a comparative pattern of writing will prevail, providing a framework for your thoughts. If your objective is to show the causes of something, perhaps a trend or an event, then a discernible pattern of causes is likely to emerge in your writing.

Patterns can help you organize your thoughts so that your audience can easily understand your message. Each pattern is a collection of strategies for achieving certain purposes. Patterns are especially useful at the workplace when you need to respond succinctly according to a company-honored format or in a college essay test when your work must be done with an oppressive clock ticking and evaluated by instructors overloaded with bluebooks.

Two cautionary points are worth considering:

- If the strategies are used in a strictly formulaic manner, the result may be mechanical and uninteresting. Fleshing out your ideas with explanation will usually submerge patterns of writing.
- It is uncommon for a single pattern to be used alone, and you would seldom attempt to do so. You cannot write a comparison-and-contrast essay without analyzing your content through division, and you might very well use definitions and examples.

Therefore, a well-written essay is usually a combination of different patterns from the ten or so available to you in narrative, descriptive,

203

expository, and persuasive writing. One form may very well provide the organizational plan for your writing, but it should not be mechanical.

This chapter presents basic strategies for using those patterns, including some general writing topics that can be used to practice the patterns.

～ Specific Patterns of Writing

Descriptive Narration

1. Include these points so that you will be sure you have a complete narrative:

   - situation (what's going on)
   - conflict (problem to be dealt with)
   - struggle (dealing with problem)
   - outcome (result of dealing with problem)
   - meaning (significance or point)

2. Use description to enhance and support your narration. A good descriptive writer presents material so that the perceptive reader can read and reexperience the writer's ideas. One device important to that writer is imagery. Images can be perceived through the senses (sight, sound, taste, smell, and touch). A good descriptive writer also gives specific details and presents concrete particulars (actual things) in a convincing way. We read, we visualize, we identify, and—*zap*—we connect with a narrative account.

3. Use dialogue as appropriate.

4. Consider using the following transitional words to improve coherence by connecting ideas with ideas, sentences with sentences, and paragraphs with paragraphs:

   - **For description—Place:** *above, over, under, below, nearby, near, across, beyond, among, to the right, to the left, in the background, in the foreground, further, beside, opposite, within sight, out of sight*
   - **For narration—Time:** *after, before, later, earlier, initially, soon, recently, next, today, tomorrow, yesterday, now, then, until, currently, when, finally, not long after, immediately, (at) first, (at) last, third, previously, in the meantime, meanwhile*

5. Give details concerning action.

6. Be consistent with point of view (use *I* for first person or *he, she,* or *it* for third person) and verb tense (use *is* for present and *was* for past).
7. Keep in mind that most narratives written as college assignments will have an expository purpose; that is, they explain a specific idea.
8. Consider working with a limited time frame for short writing assignments; that is, the scope would usually be no more than one incident of brief duration for one paragraph. For example, writing about an entire graduation ceremony might be too complicated, but concentrating on the moment when you walked forward to receive the diploma or the moment when the relatives and friends come down on the field could work very well in a single paragraph.

General Topics

Each of the following topics concerns the writing of a descriptive narrative with meaning beyond the story itself. The narrative will be used to inform or to persuade in relation to a clearly stated idea.

1. Write a narrative based on a topic sentence such as this: "One experience showed me what _____ [pain, fear, anger, love, sacrifice, dedication, joy, sorrow, shame, pride] was really like."
2. Write a simple narrative about a fire, a riot, an automobile accident, a rescue, shoplifting, or some other unusual happening you witnessed.

Exemplification

1. Use examples to explain, convince, or amuse.
2. Use examples that are vivid, specific, and representative.

   - Vivid examples (the most colorful or memorable from your list of possible examples) attract attention.
   - Specific examples (such as names of places, things, and people) are identifiable.
   - Representative examples (those that are recognizable to readers) are typical and therefore the basis for generalization.

3. Tie your examples clearly to your thesis and your main points.
4. Draw your examples from what you have read, heard, and experienced.
5. Brainstorm a list or cluster of possible examples before you write.

6. Choose the order (time, place, or emphasis) and number of your examples according to the purpose stated in your topic sentence or thesis.

7. Consider using the following transitional words to improve coherence by connecting ideas with ideas, sentences with sentences, and paragraphs with paragraphs.

  ▪ *for example, as an example, another example, for instance, such as, including, specifically, especially, in particular, to illustrate, as an illustration, that is, i.e.* (meaning *that is*), *e.g.* (meaning *for example*)

General Topics

Make a judgmental statement about an issue you believe in strongly and then use one or more examples to illustrate your point. These are some possible topics:

1. high price of groceries
2. practical car(s) for family
3. property owners with(out) pride
4. violent computer games

5. good (or bad) role model(s)
6. pet peeve: drivers who break laws
7. bad job(s)
8. true friend(s)

Analysis by Division

Almost anything can be analyzed by division—for example, how the parts of the ear work in hearing, how the parts of the eye work in seeing, or how the parts of the heart work in pumping blood throughout the body. Subjects such as these are all approached with the same systematic procedure.

1. This is the procedure.

  ▪ Step 1: Begin with something that is a unit.
  ▪ Step 2: State the principle by which the unit can function.
  ▪ Step 3: Divide the unit into parts according to that principle.
  ▪ Step 4: Discuss each of the parts in relation to the unit.

2. This is the way you might apply that procedure to a good boss.

  ▪ Unit: Manager
  ▪ Principle of function: Effective as a leader
  ▪ Parts based on the principle: Fair, intelligent, stable, competent in field
  ▪ Discussion: Consider each part in relation to the person's effectiveness as a manager.

3. This is how a basic outline of analysis by division might look.

Thesis: To be effective as a leader, a manager needs specific qualities.

I. Fairness

II. Intelligence

III. Stability

IV. Competence in the field

4. Consider using the following transitional words to improve coherence by connecting ideas with ideas, sentences with sentences, and paragraphs with paragraphs.

- **Time or Numbering:** *first, second, third, another, last, finally, soon, later, currently, before, along with, another part (section, component)*
- **Space:** *above, below, to the left, to the right, near, beyond, under, next to, in the background, split, divide*
- **Emphasis:** *most important(ly), equally important, central to the, to this end, as a result, taken collectively, with this purpose in mind, working with the, in fact, of course, above all, most of all, especially, primarily, without question*

General Topics

Some of the following topics are too broad for a short writing assignment and should be narrowed. For example, the general "a wedding ceremony" could be narrowed to the particular: José and Maria's wedding ceremony." Divide your focused topic into parts and analyze it.

1. A wedding, a graduation, a religious ceremony, a holiday, a religious revival
2. A family, a relationship, a gang, a club, a sorority, or a fraternity
3. An album, a performance, a song, a singer, an actor, a musical group
4. A movie, a television program, or a video game

Process Analysis

1. Decide whether your process analysis is mainly **directive** (how to do something) or **informative** (how you did something or how

something occurred). Be consistent in using pronouns and other designations.

- For the directive process analysis, use the second person, addressing the reader as *you*. The *you* may be understood, even if it is not written.
- For the informative process analysis, use the first person, speaking as *I* or *we*, or the third person, speaking about the subject as *he, she, it,* or *they,* or by name.

2. Consider using these basic forms:

Directive Process Analysis

I. Preparation
   A.
   B.
II. Steps
   A.
   B.
   C.

How to Prepare Spring Rolls
I. Preparation
   A. Suitable cooking area
   B. Utensils, equipment
   C. Spring-roll wrappers
   D. Vegetables, sauce
II. Steps
   A. Season vegetables
   B. Wrap vegetables
   C. Fold wrappers
   D. Deep fry rolls
   E. Serve rolls with sauce

Informative Process Analysis

I. Background
   A.
   B.
II. Sequence
   A.
   B.
   C.

How Coal Is Formed
I. Background or context
   A. Accumulation of land
      plants
   B. Bacterial action
   C. Muck formation
II. Sequence
   A. Lignite from pressure
   B. Bituminous from deep
      burial and heat
   C. Anthracite from metamor-
      phic conditions

3. Create a list, beginning with the Roman-numeral headings indicated in item 2.

4. Determine the order of process analysis. It will usually be chronological (based on time).
5. Consider using the following transitional words to improve coherence by connecting ideas with ideas, sentences with sentences, and paragraphs with paragraphs.

- **Preparation and Background:** *at the outset, before stages develop, before steps occur, before work begins, as preparation for, in anticipation of, in laying the groundwork*
- **Steps and Stages:** *first, second, third, another step, next, now, then, at this point, at this stage, at this step, after, at last, finally, subsequently, to begin with, initially, after that, afterward, at the same time, concurrently, meanwhile, soon, during the process, during . . . , in order to, for a minute, for a . . .*

General Topics

Most of the following topics are directive as they are phrased. However, each can be transformed into a how-it-was-done informative topic by personalizing it and explaining stage by stage how you, someone else, or a group did something. For example, you could write either a directive process analysis about how to deal with an obnoxious person or an informative process analysis about how you or someone else dealt with an obnoxious person. Keep in mind that the two types of process analysis are often blended, especially in the personal approach. Many of the following topics will be more interesting to you and your readers if they are personalized.

Select one of the following topics and write a process-analysis paragraph or essay about it. Most of the topics require some narrowing to be treated in a paragraph. For example, writing about playing baseball is too broad; writing about how to throw a curve ball may be manageable.

> How to pass a test for a driver's license, get a job at a specific place, cook a food, eat a food, fix an appliance, fix a sprinkler, change a tire on a car, assemble an item, wrap a package, repair clothing, perform a task at work, perform a task at home, paint a house, or change a diaper.

Cause and Effect

1. Determine whether your topic should mainly inform or mainly persuade, and use the right tone for your purpose and audience.

2. Use listing to brainstorm cause-and-effect ideas. This is an effective form of prewriting.

Causes	Event, Situation, or Trend	Effects
Low self-esteem	*Joining a gang*	Life of crime
Drugs		Drug addiction
Tradition		Surrogate family
Fear		relationship
Needs surrogate family		Protection
Wants protection		Ostracism
Neighborhood status		Restricted vocational
		opportunities

3. Decide whether to concentrate on causes, effects, or a combination of causes and effects. Most paragraphs will focus only on causes or only on effects. Many short essays will discuss causes and effects but will use one as the framework for the piece. A typical basic outline might look like this:

Topic sentence of paragraph or thesis of essay
   I. Cause (or Effect) 1
  II. Cause (or Effect) 2
 III. Cause (or Effect) 3

4. Do not conclude that something is an effect merely because it follows something else. For example, a recession after the election of a new leader may or may not be an effect of the election.
5. Lend emphasis to your main concern(s)—causes, effects, or a combination—by repeating key words such as *cause, reason, effect, result, consequence,* and *outcome.*
6. Keep in mind that causes and effects can be primary (main) or secondary (contributing), immediate or remote.
7. Base the order of causes and effects in your paper on time, space, emphasis, or a combination.
8. Consider using the following transitional words to improve coherence by connecting ideas with ideas, sentences with sentences, and paragraphs with paragraphs.

- **Cause:** *as, because, because of, due to, for, for the reason that, since, bring about, another cause, for this reason, one cause, a second cause, another cause, a final cause*
- **Effect:** *accordingly, finally, consequently, hence, so, therefore, thus, as a consequence, as a result, resulting*

General Topics

Select one of the topics in the following list as a subject (situation, circumstance, or trend) for your paragraph or essay and then determine whether you will concentrate on causes, effects, or a combination. You can probably write a more interesting, well-developed, and therefore successful paragraph or essay on a topic you can personalize. If you do not personalize the topic, you will probably have to do some basic research to supply details for development.

1. attending or completing college
2. change in policy at work or school
3. alcoholism, any addiction
4. moving to another country, state, or home
5. passing or failing a test or course
6. having or getting a job
7. change in coaches, teachers
8. gambling
9. exercising, dieting
10. teenage marriage or parenthood

Comparison and Contrast

One useful procedure for writing comparison-and-contrast paragraphs and essays is using the 4 *P*'s: *purpose, points, patterns,* and *presentation.*

1. **Purpose:** During the exploration of your topic, define your purpose clearly.

   - Decide whether you are writing a work that is primarily comparison, primarily contrast, or balanced.
   - Determine whether your main purpose is to inform or to persuade. For example, you might argue that one minivan is better than another.

2. Points

- Indicate your points of comparison or contrast, perhaps by listing.
- Eliminate irrelevant points.

  horsepower and gears

  ~~safety~~

  style

  ~~price~~

  ~~comfort~~

  cargo space

3. Pattern

- Select the subject-by-subject or the point-by-point pattern after considering your topic and planned treatment. The point-by-point pattern is usually preferred in essays. Only in long papers is there likely to be a mixture of patterns.
- Compose an outline reflecting the pattern you select.

Subject-by-Subject Pattern

I. Subject 1
   A. Point 1
   B. Point 2
II. Subject 2
   A. Point 1
   B. Point 2

I. Nissan Quest
   A. Horsepower and gears
   B. Safety
   C. Cargo space
II. Dodge Caravan
   A. Horsepower and gears
   B. Safety
   C. Cargo space

Point-by-Point Pattern

I. Point 1
   A. Subject 1
   B. Subject 2
II. Point 2
   A. Subject 1
   B. Subject 2
III. Point 3
   A. Subject 1
   B. Subject 2

I. Horsepower and gears
   A. Nissan Quest
   B. Dodge Caravan
II. Safety
   A. Nissan Quest
   B. Dodge Caravan
III. Cargo space
   A. Nissan Quest
   B. Dodge Caravan

4. **Presentation:** Give each point more or less equal treatment. Attention to each part of the outline will usually ensure balanced development.
5. Use a carefully stated topic sentence for a paragraph and a clear thesis for an essay. Each developmental paragraph should have a topic sentence broad enough to embrace its content.
6. Consider using the following transitional words to improve coherence by connecting ideas with ideas, sentences with sentences, and paragraphs with paragraphs.

- **Comparison:** *in the same way, similarly, likewise, also, by comparison, in a like manner, as, with, as though, both, like, just as*
- **Contrast:** *but, by contrast, in contrast, despite, however, instead, nevertheless, on (to) the contrary, in spite of, still, yet, unlike, even so, rather than, otherwise*

General Topics

Make these topics specific by naming the subjects for your comparison and contrast.

1. Two products, such as automobiles, bicycles, or motorcycles
2. Two types of (or specific) police officers, doctors, teachers, clergy, students, or athletes
3. Two roommates, neighbors, friends, or dates
4. Two movies, television shows, commercials, songs, or singers
5. Dating and going steady, living together and being married, or a person before and after marriage

Definition

Simple Definition

1. Keep in mind that no two words have exactly the same meaning.
2. Blend any of several forms of simple definitions into your discussion: basic dictionary definitions, synonyms, direct explanations, indirect explanations, and analytical definitions.
3. For a formal or an analytical definition, specify the term, class, and characteristic(s).

EXAMPLE Capitalism is an economic system characterized by investment
        term   class
of money, private ownership, and free enterprise.
                characteristics

4. Avoid "is where" and "is when" definitions, circular definitions, and the use of words in the definition that are more difficult than the word being defined.

Extended Definition

1. Use listing or clustering to consider how you might use other patterns of development in defining your term. (See page 215.)
2. Decide how you will organize your writing. The organization of your extended definition is likely to be one of emphasis, but it may also be one of space or time, depending on the subject material. You may use just one pattern of development for the overall organization.
3. Consider these ways of introducing a definition: with a question, with a statement of what it is not, with a statement of what it originally meant, or with a discussion of why a clear definition is important. You may use a combination of these ways before you continue with your definition.
4. Consider your purpose and your audience to determine whether you will personalize a definition. Your instructor may ask you to write about a word within the context of your own experience or to write about it from a detached, clinical viewpoint.
5. Consider using the following transitional words to improve coherence by connecting ideas with ideas, sentences with sentences, and paragraphs with paragraphs.

   - *originates from, means, derives from, refers to, for example, as a term, as a concept, label, similar to, different from, in a particular context, in common usage, in historical context*

General Topics

The following topics are appropriate for extended development of definitions; most of them will also serve well for writing simple definitions.

1. role model
2. hero
3. happiness
4. cult
5. psychopath
6. successful
7. workaholic
8. street smart

9. brave
10. educated
11. cool
12. love

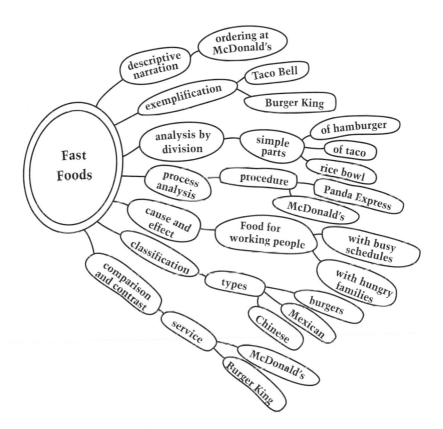

Argument

1. Ask yourself the following questions. Then consider which parts of the formal argument you should include in your paragraph or essay.

   - **Background:** What is the historical or social context for this controversial issue?
   - **Proposition** (the **thesis** of the essay): What do I want my audience to believe or to do?

- **Qualification of proposition:** Can I limit my proposition so that those who disagree cannot easily challenge me with exceptions?
- **Refutation** (taking the opposing view into account, mainly to point out its fundamental weakness): What is the view on the other side, and why is it flawed in reasoning or evidence?
- **Support:** In addition to sound reasoning, can I use appropriate facts, examples, statistics, and opinions of authorities?

2. The basic pattern of a paragraph or an essay of argument is likely to be in this form:

Proposition (the thesis of the essay)

I. Support 1
II. Support 2
III. Support 3

3. Consider using the following transitional words to improve coherence by connecting ideas with ideas, sentences with sentences, and paragraphs with paragraphs.

- *it follows that, as a result, causes taken collectively, as a concession, even though, of course, in the context of, in the light of, in the final analysis, following this, further, as additional support, moreover, consequently, according to, in support of, contrary to, therefore, naturally*

General Topics

The following are broad subject areas; you will have to limit your focus for an essay of argument. You may modify the topics to fit specific situations. Consider using examples.

1. Juvenile justice, treating youngsters as adults in courts
2. Advertising tobacco, alcohol, and other drugs
3. Casinos and state-run lotteries
4. Laws for those who do graffiti in public places
5. Smoking in public places: restaurants, bars, parks
6. Drivers licenses for the young and the old
7. Surveillance by video (on campus, in classrooms, in neighborhoods, or in shopping areas)
8. Curfew for teenagers
9. Laws requiring residents to maintain appearance of property
10. Keeping gang members out of parks

⌒ A Variety of Writing Topics

Here are some paragraph and essay topics. For each topic that you choose, try one or more prewriting techniques, such as brainstorming, freewriting, or clustering. Then develop a strong topic sentence and a clear outline before you write, revise, and edit your paper.

1. Write about the best or the worst decision you made during the past three years.
2. Write about the breakup of a relationship. Concentrate on causes or effects.
3. Write about people's driving habits that bother you. Give some real-life examples.
4. Bring in a newspaper article of opinion (often located on the page facing the editorial page) or a letter to the editor and then agree or disagree with it in a very specific way.
5. Write your own letter to an editor of a newspaper about an issue in the news. Consider mailing your letter.
6. Write about needed changes in procedures, management, products, or services in your workplace.
7. Write about an imaginary vacation to a time and place of your choice in world history (no space alien abduction pieces unless approved by your instructor).
8. Imagine that you have just won a million dollars in the lottery. Explain what you would do. Be specific in naming products and beneficiaries.
9. Write your job description (what you are supposed to do) in one paragraph, explaining each task as a part of your total job, and then, in an additional paragraph, explain what you really do.
10. Discuss a personal hero or role model. Emphasize the important qualities of that person.
11. Summarize a passage from a college textbook. When you summarize a passage, you rewrite it, making it shorter by about two-thirds, changing the wording without changing the information, and concentrating on main ideas. Do not add ideas, refer to yourself (by using "I"), or give your opinion. Begin by underlining the important ideas and annotating the printed material. Then construct a simple outline. Try referring only to your outline to avoid the temptation of copying material.
12. Write a detailed account of how someone helped you at a time when your self-esteem was low.

13. If you are from an immigrant family, write about what happened when your family learned about American culture by watching television soon after you arrived in this country.
14. Write about the effects television watching has had on you. How has your life changed by the amount of TV viewing you do and by your choice of programs?
15. Use the Internet to research the price, quality, style, and durability of two items that are for sale. Make copies of your data. Write a comparison-and-contrast paper explaining that one item is better than the other. Submit the computer printout along with the materials required by your instructor.
16. Write an argument either for or against the practice of using cameras in classrooms to help control bullying, cheating, bad teaching, and thefts.
17. Imagine you are leaving a job without being able to give notification. Your respected—and understanding—boss asks you to write out instructions in short essay form to help your replacement perform a task.
18. Write about a workaholic (a person who places work above all other activities and concerns) you know. Emphasize either the effects on that person and his or her family or the causes of the person's becoming fanatical about work.
19. Use one extended example of someone who is a good boss, worker, parent, coach, spouse, or neighbor.
20. Write about a crime, an accident, or a natural disaster you witnessed.

Index

a/an/and, 185
a/an/the, 2, 4
abbreviations
  capitalizing, 173
  punctuating, 152, 155
accept/except, 185–186
action verbs, 3, 17
active voice, 112–113
addresses, punctuating, 156
adjectives, 4, 136
  commas with, 154
  comparative and superlative forms,
    140–141
  confused with adverbs, 141–142
adverbs, 4–5, 136
  beginning sentences with, 54
  comparative and superlative forms,
    141–142
  confused with adjectives, 141–142
  prepositional phrases as, 6
  selecting, 138–139
advice/advise, 186
all ready/already, 186
all right/alright, 186
a lot/alot, 186
alternative subjects
  pronoun-antecedent agreement
    and, 128–129
  subject-verb agreement and, 105
altogether/all together, 186
analysis by division, 206–207
apostrophes, 171–172
appositive phrases, 50, 62, 169
argument, 215–216
articles, 2, 4

bad/badly, 141
being verbs, 3, 17, 114, 120
both/and, 7, 82
brackets, 170
brainstorming, 195, 205, 210

capitalization, 172–174, 198
case, pronoun, 118–122
cause and effect, 209–211
choose/chose, 186
clauses, 6, 27–29, 103, 119, 153
  See also dependent clauses;
    independent clauses
CLUESS acronym, for revision
  process, 198
clustering, 195, 196, 214, 215
coherence
  in revision process, 198
  transitional words for, 204, 206, 207,
    209, 210–211, 213, 214, 216
collective nouns
  pronoun-antecedent agreement
    and, 129
  subject-verb agreement and, 105
colons, 169–170
  with parentheses, 170
  quotation marks and, 166
commas, 153–156
  for comma splices and run-ons, 68
  in complex sentences, 32, 45–46
  with coordinating conjunctions, 31,
    39, 153
  with parentheses, 170
  quotation marks and, 155, 166
  for sentence fragments, 61
  to separate, 153–154
  in series, 154, 160
  to set off, 154–156
  with subordinating conjunctions, 7,
    45–46
comma splices, 67–75
  coordinating conjunctions for, 68
  making separate sentences for,
    74–75
  semicolons for, 73
  subordinating conjunctions for,
    70–71

community dialects, vs. standard
    usage, 93–95
comparative modifiers, 140–142
comparison and contrast, 211–213
complete subjects, 12
complex sentences, 27, 29
    defined, 32–33, 53
    punctuation in, 32, 45–46
    relative pronouns in, 45–46
    subordinating conjunctions in, 45–46
    for subordination of ideas, 43–46
compound-complex sentences, 27, 29
    for coordination and subordination
        of ideas, 48–49
    defined, 33–34, 53
    punctuation in, 49
compound sentences, 27, 29
    conjunctive adverbs in, 41–42
    for coordination of ideas, 38–42
    defined, 31–32, 53
    punctuation in, 31, 39, 41–42
compound subjects, 14
    determining pronoun case with, 121
    pronoun-antecedent agreement
        and, 128
    subject-verb agreement and, 103,
        104–105
concrete particulars, 204
conjunctions, 6–8
    confused with prepositions, 8
    paired, 7
    See also coordinating conjunctions;
        subordinating conjunctions
conjunctive adverbs
    beginning sentences with, 54
    for comma splices and run-ons, 73
    common, 42, 73
    in compound sentences, 41–42
    HOTSHOT CAT acronym for, 42,
        73, 160
    punctuation with, 41–42, 155, 160
contractions, 171–172
coordinating conjunctions, 7
    beginning sentences with, 54
    for comma splices and run-ons, 68
    in compound sentences, 31, 38–39
    FANBOYS acronym for, 7, 31,
        38–39, 68

parallel structure and, 81
punctuation with, 31, 39, 153,
    154, 160
coordination
    compound-complex sentences for,
        48–49
    compound sentences for, 38–42
COPS acronym, for editing, 198
could of/could have, 186

dangling modifiers, 146
dashes, 168–169
    quotation marks and, 166
dates, commas with, 155
definition, 213–214
dependent clauses, 6, 27–28
    beginning sentences with, 54
    in complex sentences, 32
    as sentence fragments, 60–61
    using commas with, 7, 45–46, 153
descriptive narration, 204–205
dialogue
    in description, 204
    quotation marks for, 165
    using dashes in, 169
diction, impact of modifiers on, 138
directive process analysis, 207, 208
direct objects, 91–92, 120
direct quotations, 164–165
double negatives, 141

editing process, 198–200
effect/affect, 186
either/or, 7
    as parallel structure signal, 82
    pronoun-antecedent agreement
        and, 128–129
    subject-verb agreement and, 105
ellipsis, 152
emphasis
    repeating key words for, 210
    in revision process, 198
emphatic statements, punctuating, 169
end punctuation, 152–153
essays, 193
    common patterns for, 203–216
    writing topics for, 217–218
    See also writing process

exclamation points, 153
  in interjections, 8
  parentheses and, 170
  quotation marks and, 166
exclamations, 62
exemplification, 205–206
expository writing, 205
extended definitions, 214

FANBOYS acronym, 7, 31, 38–39, 68
fragments, sentence, 59–63
freewriting, 194–195

gerund phrases, 28
gerunds, 18
good/well, 141
greetings, 63

hear/here, 186
helping verbs, 3, 17
here/there, 15, 104
HOTSHOT CAT acronym, 12, 73, 160
hyphens, 172

imagery, in description, 204
imperative sentences, 14
implied subjects, 14, 62
indefinite pronouns, 2, 13
  possessive form of, 171
  pronoun-antecedent agreement
    and, 128, 129–130
  subject-verb agreement and, 104
  See also pronouns
independent clauses, 6, 27
  in comma splices and run-ons, 67–75
  joining in compound sentences, 31,
    38–39, 41
  using semicolons with, 31, 41, 160
indirect objects, 120
interjections, 8, 62, 155
introductory elements, commas
    with, 153
introductory paragraphs, 193
inversions, and subject-verb
    agreement, 104
irregular verbs, 88–91
italics, 166–167
it's/its, 186

know/no, 187

language, in revision process, 198
led/lead, 187
let's, 122
letters, punctuating, 156, 169 170
lie/lay, 91–92
lists, punctuating, 168, 169
loose/lose, 187

me/I, 121
misplaced modifiers, 146–147
modifiers, 146–147
  See also adjectives; adverbs

names and titles, capitalizing, 174
narration, 204–205
neither/nor, 7
  as parallel structure signal, 82
  pronoun-antecedent agreement
    and, 128–129
  subject-verb agreement and, 105
never/not/hardly, 19
not only/but also
  as parallel structure signal, 82
  pronoun-antecedent agreement
    and, 128–129
  subject-verb agreement and, 105
noun indicators, 2, 4
nouns, 2, 13
  as antecedents, 126–130
  capitalizing proper, 173
  collective, 105, 129
  direct address, 155
  possessive form of, 171
  subject-verb agreement and,
    105, 106
number agreement
  of pronouns and antecedents, 127,
    128–129
  of subjects and verbs, 103–106
numbers
  punctuating, 155, 156, 172
  subject-verb agreement with,
    105–106

objective case, of pronouns, 120–121
omissions, 51–52, 198

outlines
  for analysis by division, 207
  in writing process, 194, 196

paid/payed, 187
paragraphs, 193
  common patterns for, 203–216
  topic sentence of, 193, 195
  writing topics for, 217–218
  See also writing process
parallelism, 79–80
parentheses, 170
parenthetical elements, commas
      for, 155
participial phrases, 28
  for combining sentences, 51
participles, 18–19
parts of speech, 1–11
passed/past, 187
passive voice, 112–113
past participles, 88, 89–91
past tense, 86, 87, 89, 92, 109
patience/patients, 187
patterns of writing. *See* writing
      patterns
peace/piece, 187
phrases, 28, 60, 61–62, 103
  compared with clauses, 28
  defined, 6
  introductory, commas with, 153
  wordy, 191
point-by-point pattern, in
      comparison and contrast, 212
point of view, in descriptive
      narration, 205
possessives, apostrophes for, 171
prepositional phrases, 28
  beginning sentences with, 54, 61
  for combining sentences, 51
  confusing with subject, 14–15
  defined, 5, 6
  passive voice and, 112, 113
  as sentence fragments, 61
prepositions, 5–6, 8
  avoiding omission of, 52
  common, 6, 14
  object of, 5, 6, 14–15, 121
  subject-verb agreement and, 103

present tense, 86, 92
  of irregular verbs, 89
  for literature, 109
  of regular verbs, 86–87
prewriting stage, 194–197
process analysis, 207–209
progressive tenses, 93
pronouns, 2–3, 13
  agreement with antecedents, 126–130
  case of, 118–122
  common problems with, 118
  gender agreement of, 129–130
  indefinite, 13
  number agreement of, 128–129
  objective case of, 120–121
  person agreement of, 127
  personal, 13
  possessive form of, 171
  references, avoiding unclear, 132–133
  relative, 28, 45–46
  subjective case of, 119–120
  subject-verb agreement and, 104
  techniques for determining case of,
        121–122
punctuation, 198
  apostrophes, 171–172
  brackets, 170
  colons, 169–170
  commas, 153–156
  for comma splices and run-ons, 68
  in complete sentences, 59
  in complex sentences, 32, 45–46
  in compound-complex sentences, 49
  in compound sentences, 31, 39,
        41–42
  with conjunctive adverbs, 41–42
  with coordinating conjunctions, 31,
        39, 153, 154, 160
  dashes, 168–169
  end, 152–153
  hyphens, 172
  italics, 166–167
  parentheses, 170
  quotation marks, 164–166
  with relative pronouns, 46
  semicolons, 160
  with subordinating conjunctions,
        7, 45–46

question marks, 153
  parentheses and, 170
  quotation marks and, 166
questions
  as acceptable fragments, 63
  for brainstorming, 195
  colons with, 169
  pronouns introducing, 3, 13
quiet/quit/quite, 187
quotation marks, 164–166
  punctuation with, 155, 166
quotations
  brackets in, 170
  colons with, 169
  within quotations, 165

real/really, 141
receive/recieve, 187
regular verbs, 86–88
relative clauses, 28, 32, 45–46, 60–61
relative pronouns, 28, 45–46
representative examples, 205
revision process, 198–200
rise/raise, 91–92
run-ons, 67–75

semicolons, 160
  for comma splices and run-ons, 73
  in compound complex sentences, 49
  in compound sentences,
    31, 41–42
  conjunctive adverbs and, 41–42
  with parentheses, 170
  quotation marks and, 166
sentences
  balancing, 79–82
  clauses in, 27–29
  combining. *See* sentences,
    combining
  comma splices and run-ons
    in, 67–75
  complex, 32–33
  compound, 31–32
  compound-complex, 33–34
  fragments, 59–63
  in revision process, 198
  simple, 30
  topic, 193, 194, 195

types of, 29–34, 53
  wordy phrases in, 191
sentences, combining
  avoiding omissions, 51–52
  coordination, 38–42
  coordination and subordination,
    48–49
  other methods, 50–51
  subordination, 43–46
sentence variety
  beginnings, 54
  length, 54
  order of parts for, 54
  types of sentences, 29–34, 53
series
  comma use in, 154
  semicolon use in, 160
sex bias, 130
simple sentences, 27, 29, 30, 38, 53
simple subjects, 12
simple tenses, 92
sit/set, 91–92
slang, quotation marks for, 165
specific examples, 205
spelling, 198
  frequently misspelled words,
    182–183
  misspelled/confusing words,
    185–188
  tips for, 179–182
standard usage, of verbs, 86, 93–95
stationary/stationery, 187–188
strong verbs, 114
subject-by-subject pattern, in
    comparison and contrast, 212
subjective case, of pronouns,
    119–120
subjects, 12–15
  agreement with verbs, 103–106
  alternative, 105, 128–129
  avoiding omission of, 51, 62
subordinating conjunctions, 7
  for comma splices and run-ons,
    70–71
  in complex sentences, 45–46
  list of, 7, 28, 45, 71
  punctuation with, 7, 45–46
  in sentence fragments, 60

subordination
  complex sentence for, 43–46
  compound-complex sentences for,
    48–49
suffixes, adding, 181–182
superlative modifiers, 140–142
support
  in argument, 216
  in outlines, 196
  in paragraphs, 193
  in revision process, 198

technical terms, quotation marks
    for, 165
tenses. *See* verb tenses
than/then, 188
that, avoiding omission of, 52
their/there/they're, 188
there/here, 15, 104
thesaurus, 139
thorough/through, 188
titles of works
  capitalizing, 174
  italicizing, 166–167
  quotation marks for, 165
  subject-verb agreement and, 105
topics, for writing, 205, 206, 207, 209,
    211, 213, 214, 216, 217–218
topic sentence, 193, 194, 195
to/too/two, 188
transitional words
  for coherence, 204, 206, 207, 209,
    210–211, 213, 214, 216
truly/truely, 188

unity, in revision process, 198

verbals, 18–19, 28, 51
  as sentence fragments, 61
verbs, 17–19
  action, 3, 17
  active and passive voice of, 112–113
  agreement with subjects, 103–106
  avoiding omission of, 51–52, 62
  being, 3, 17, 114, 120
  community dialects and, 93–95
verb tenses, 3, 86
  consistency in, 108–109
  of irregular verbs, 88–91
  kinds of, 92–93
  of regular verbs, 86–88
vivid examples, 205

weather/whether, 188
whether/or
  as parallel structure signal, 82
  pronoun-antecedent agreement
    and, 128–129
who/whom, 46, 121–122
wordy phrases, 191
writer's block, 194
write/writen/written, 188
writing patterns, 203–216
writing process, 193–201
  general description of, 194
  paragraphs and essays, 193
  prewriting stage, 194–197
  revising and editing, 198–200
  topics for, 217–218
  writing first draft, 197–198
  writing process worksheet, 201–202

you're/your, 188